Buffalo Bill Historical Center, Cody, Wyoming, U.S.A.; Gift of J.W. Duke Wellington, NA.203.334
Warbonnet from Ft. Belknap Reservation, ca. 1920

The Plains Warbonnet
Its Story and Construction

By Barry E. Hardin

Author's Forward

Since the earliest European contacts and continuing through today, the American Indian has been an object of fascination, both on this continent and around the world. However, from the beginning, Indian cultures have widely been misunderstood and misinterpreted. Even today, after much study and enlightenment, there is ignorance and misinformation about these peoples who continue to live among us. As a reflection of this lack of understanding, the warbonnet has become the symbol most identified by the public with all Native Americans, regardless of their particular tribe or culture.

This book is an attempt to bring together a number of aspects pertaining to the warbonnet. Though it is far from comprehensive, the topics addressed include the history, uses, and meanings of the warbonnet for those who made and used them. We also observe that, by the mid-1800s, a number of styles had been developed, and the wide access to trade goods by Indians was reflected in the kinds of decorative materials found on most warbonnet specimens. Even today, the warbonnet continues to evolve.

A large portion of the book gives details on constructing a 'typical" Plains warbonnet and variations that might be considered when making a recreation of this widely-used piece of headgear. However, by becoming aware of the breadth of the warbonnet topic, it is hoped that this book will inspire craftsmen to more thoroughly study warbonnets, as well as heighten their appreciation of the broader story and significance.

The author is indebted to those ethnographers and scholars who heretofore have researched and unearthed information that has added to the warbonnet's story. Yet, there still are many details that have not been discovered and perhaps never will. However, we hope that, among the readers, there will be some who continue the search for knowledge about this fascinating subject and add more chapters at some future date.

This book is dedicated to the late Frank Knickerbocker, my dear friend and first true mentor. It was Frank who took out his early Kiowa warbonnet and began to reveal to me, a young novice, its many mysteries.

Barry Hardin
November, 2012

Publication Credits

Published by: Crazy Crow Trading Post P.O. Box 847 • Pottsboro, TX 75076 • (903) 786-2287 www.crazycrow.com

Cover Design: Michael A. Catellier

Cover Photo: Sioux bonnet with quilled brow band. Buffalo Bill Historical Center, Cody, Wyoming, U.S.A.; Gift of Irving H. "Larry" Larom Estate, NA.205.35

Designed by: Michael A. Catellier, Barry Hardin and J. Rex Reddick

Graphic Designer & Illustrated by: Michael A. Catellier and Barry Hardin

ISBN 1-929572-23-9

©Copyright 2013 Crazy Crow Trading Post
All rights reserved. No part of this publication may be reproduced or transmitted in any form of by any means, electronic or mechanical, including photocopying, recording or any information storage and retrieval system, without written permission from the publisher.

Table of Contents

1. Introduction: How To Use This Booklet — 5
2. The Plains Warbonnet in History — 7
3. Significance: Myth and Reality — 13
4. Acquiring Feathers — 15
5. The Story Behind the Warbonnet — 17
6. Plains Bonnet Styles — 25
7. Materials & Construction Basics: An Overview — 39
8. A Note About Photographs — 63
9. Construction Of The Basic Warbonnet — 65
    - Materials
    - Crown
    - Brow band
    - Drops &/or Beaded Rosettes
    - Feather Preparation
    - Bonnet Assembly
10. Trailer Bonnets: Materials & Construction — 97
11. Straight Up Bonnets: Materials & Construction — 105
12. Summary — 115
13. Photo Gallery — 116
14. Acknowledgements   Bibliographyy — 128

Buffalo Bill Historical Center, Cody, Wyoming, U.S.A.; The Crow Indian Collection of Dr. William and Anna Petzolt, Gift of the Genevieve Fitzgerald Estate, NA.203.934.

Warbonnet of immature golden eagle feathers collected from White Man Runs Him, Crow, in the early 1900's

Introduction 1

The Plains Indians' feathered warbonnet is arguably the most recognized material symbol of the Native American. From earliest European contact, the term "warbonnet" appears numerous times throughout literature relating to indigenous peoples. However, it is a somewhat general term used to refer to any one of the numerous tribal and personal variants of men's headdresses. And so the term is imprecise and readily misunderstood, particularly because early historians and observers who placed the term in common usage did not yet appreciate the cultural and religious significance of these and so many other objects of Native manufacture.

For our purpose, the word "warbonnet" refers to a skull cap decorated with a circle of eagle feathers. In the following discussion, we also will substitute the words "bonnet" and "headdress" to mean the same thing. In addition, the term will include warbonnets with one or two "trailers" of feathers attached to a panel extending down the wearer's back.

How to Use This Book

This booklet provides instructions on how to make a basic warbonnet, plus Double and Single Trailer variations. However, as with so many Indian items, there are tribal differences and individual variations that need to be studied and appreciated. If you wish to make an authentic bonnet, we invite you to dig deeper than the basic instructions. For starters, read the discussions that precede the Construction Information for more of the history and details concerning these important symbols of the Plains Indian warrior. Further, seek out any of the numerous books on Plains Indians that include old photos taken during the 1800s and early 1900s showing Indians wearing warbonnets. Also, we are fortunate that, today, there are digital images of actual old warbonnets on museum web sites and internet links to collectors' galleries. The more you see and study the images, the more you will appreciate the sometimes subtle differences between specimens which make each one unique. And consider this: The amount of time spent making an "average" warbonnet will approximately equal what it takes to make a nice, historically accurate bonnet. The difference is that, by doing a bit of research, you will be more likely to produce a warbonnet that is authentic in many details, as well as a product of which you will be most proud.

Beinecke Rare Book and Manuscript Library, Yale University

Wolf Eagle, Blackfoot. Hand-colored glass lantern slide by Walter McClintock, ca 1900.

Denver Public Library, Western History Collection

6 Sitting Bull, Hunkpapa Sioux, poses with Buffalo Bill Cody. For a time, Sitting Bull appeared in Buffalo Bill's Wild West Show.

Above Right: Men On Horseback   Beinecke 1048987
Blackfoot men on horseback. Hand-colored glass lantern slide by Walter McClintock, ca 1900.

Beinecke Rare Book and Manuscript Library, Yale University

The Plains Warbonnet in History 2

The warbonnet is, of course, the classic American Indian headdress. Seen in wear today by a great number of tribes throughout the country, it has become synonymous with the Native American, regardless of his tribal affiliation. Although this was not always so, the Plains warbonnet has been adopted for wear by many diverse Indian culture groups in modern times, beginning in the late reservation period (ca. 1890). Originally indigenous only to the tribes of the Plains and their neighbors in the Plateau region, its popularity probably was first spread by the traveling Wild West Shows of the time, such as those of Buffalo Bill and Pawnee Bill. **(See photo pg. 6)** These men took troops of performers to the populous Eastern states and abroad to several European countries. The performers included actual Plains Indians wearing traditional regalia, and so Easterners and Europeans associated the warbonnets they saw with all Indians of North America. After all, many non-Indians – then and even today – assumed that all Indians are alike: speaking the same language, living in tipis, and sharing the same religious and material cultures.

By the early 1900s, the major railroads also had established routes across the American west and southwest, and they needed customers. As part of their advertising, they featured images of Plains Indians in native dress that the tourist could expect to see. The Indians, recognizing the economic opportunity to be derived from tourist dollars, played to that concept of what an Indian should look like by dressing in the Plains style. As a result, Indian tribes who had never had the feathered warbonnet made or acquired Plains Indians' attire – particularly the warbonnet – and performed "war dances" for the travelers. Unfortunately, the warbonnets, leggings, moccasins, and other articles they often wore were not part of their own cultures. Striking evidence of this phenomenon can be seen on postcards and snapshots of the era showing Pueblo Indians doing "war dances" and "rain dances", adorned in Plains clothing. **(See top photo, pg. 8)**

In 1964, noted authority John Ewers wrote: "… the phenomenal success of Buffalo Bill's Wild West Show encouraged others to organize similar shows which, together with small scale Indian "medicine" shows, toured the country and the Canadian provinces in the early years of the present century, giving employment to Indians who were not members of Plains tribes. These shows played a definite role in diffusing such Plains Indian traits as the flowing feather bonnet, the tipi, and the war dances of the Plains tribes to Indians who lived at a very considerable distance from the Great Plains. A Cheyenne Indian who traveled with a medicine show is reputed to have introduced the warbonnet among the Indians of Cape Breton Island [Nova Scotia] as early as the 1890s.

Author's Collection

Postcard CA. 1930. Pueblo or possibly Ute Indians wearing Lakota dance regalia.

Contacts with the Plains Indian showmen at the Pan American Exposition in Buffalo [New York] during 1901 encouraged the Seneca Indians to substitute their traditional crown of upright feathers and to learn to ride and dance like the Plains Indians so that they could obtain employment with the popular shows of the period."

Early History: Evolution and Distribution

At the time of first European contact, the Delaware Indians wore one or two rows of turkey or heron feathers in a head wrapping (possibly like a yarn sash turban). Early drawings by LaMoine (ca. 1560) show the headpiece of Timucan Indians which consisted of feathers arranged around a simple headband. (See Illustration, Page 9)

Wm. T. Bradley, an Algonquin photographed in the early 1900s. His headdress style is little changed from early European contact.

Wm. T. Bradley – **Wisconsin Historical Society, 27168**

Spanish engraving ca. 1560 of Timucan chief and his men entitled "Saturiba Goes To War." *Author's Collection*

One theory suggests that these people, who lived on the Florida peninsula, may have been a splinter group from the Mayans of Mexico. Illustrations of the elaborate and colorful headpieces worn by the Maya are well known to students of Native American material culture. To the earliest Europeans, these various headdresses seemed to have a similar appearance, if not construction. These are examples of observations that establish that, at the time of first contact, many different tribal groups from New England to Florida were wearing some type of headdress consisting of a band or wrapping which supported feathers in a vertical position. Of course, it also is likely that independant parallel development of headdress styles occurred in other parts of North America.

As early traders and trappers journeyed from the East to West, they continued to note that some Indians wore a type of headband with feathers inserted vertically. This headdress either partially or completely encircled the head, and examples apparently were more prominent in the Algonquian tribes. With the expansion of encroaching settlers, several Algonquian groups migrated West, taking their rich culture with them, and this included the headdress just described. This quite possibly was the forerunner of the warbonnet, and traces of this early style of headpiece remained in the Eastern Woodlands until about 1890.

The warbonnet as we have defined it above was reported by travelers among upper Missouri River tribes in the late 1700s. Francois LaRocque, who explored the Upper Missouri/Yellowstone area during 1804-05 and wrote the first authoritative account of the Crows, reported that they wore a "feather belt" on their heads. By the 1830s, artists traveling to the Upper Missouri were recording examples of warbonnets being worn by several tribes, including Sioux, Mandan, Pawnees, and others. See the paintings of George Bird King, George Catlin, Karl Bodmer, and other contemporaries.

Petalesharro by Charles Bird King, ca. 1822, access. no. 2126.1814.23C from the collection of Gilcrease Museum, Tulsa, Oklahoma.

Left Photo

This is one of several likenesses painted of the famous Pawnee warrior, Petalesharro. Objects in many early paintings of Native Americans, like these warbonnet feathers, were not always accurately depicted to scale.

On the Plains, the references, illustrations, and early photos of Indians in the first half of the 1800s appear to give evidence that the warbonnet was not commonplace among all tribes at that time. The Comanches, for example, recall that only a few, select warriors had the right to own a warbonnet. The oldest known warbonnet specimen in the familiar style was collected in 1838 by a Col. Swords, and it can be assumed that it was somewhat older than its collection date.

Throughout history, many of mankind's inventions seem to appear in different cultures within a fairly short time of each other, independent of outside influences. So, not surprisingly, we learn that, in pre-horse times, many of the Plateau tribes created headbands with upright eagle feathers. The Plains style bonnet seems to have been picked up by tribes such as the Flathead, Nez Perce, and others after they acquired the horse and began interacting more with other buffalo hunting tribes.

As early as 1805, the Flatheads, Shoshonis, Crows, and others attended large trade gatherings together. Warbonnets from the Plains were part of this trade economy and commanded high prices. Consequently, during the 1800s, the Plains styles replaced more traditional styles among the Plateau people. For example, by the mid-1800s, the Nez Perce had adopted the Sioux style warbonnet, and it replaced "...nearly all aboriginal styles of prestigious headwear."

Like most Indian material culture categories, the warbonnet evolved over the years. This included adding more decorations and refinements until the warbonnet as we know it today came into existence. Some of the cultures themselves changed so that it became acceptable for more men within a tribe to wear it. And, even during the late 1800s reservation period, tribes that formerly had not used the warbonnet adopted it into their own material culture.

Beinecke Rare Book and Manuscript Library, Yale University
Two Bears, Blackfoot, in eagle feather bonnet. Hand-colored glass lantern slide by Walter McClintock, ca 1900.

Significance: Myth and Reality 3

Although certain stylistic details of the basic warbonnet have evolved, one aspect did not change. From its origins and while the last survivors of Plains warfare survived, the warbonnet represented one overriding concept: bravery. Thus, a man who wore and/or owned a warbonnet was considered to be – and expected to be – brave. Even today, some tribes still associate the wearing of a warbonnet with prestige, leadership and, in many cases, being a military veteran. The old Comanches stated that a warbonnet could only be worn "in times of danger".

For a moment, we should mention that, although there are cultural differences between tribes, it also is true that those who shared particular geographical regions experienced cross-cultural influences. These appear as similarities in construction and craft techniques of material objects, ceremonies, taboos, religious beliefs and practices, and other basic cultural elements. Accordingly, we can safely generalize on certain aspects when speaking of those tribes that are considered to be Plains Indians. Thus, an examination of the warbonnet's place in the individual tribes demonstrates that the concept of bravery was associated universally with the warbonnet.

One of the commonalities of Native Americans is that few things are arbitrary. One must have or earn the right to have or do many of the things in his culture. For example, a man cannot just decide he wants a warbonnet, then make or buy one; he must "have the right".

For many Plains tribes, each feather in a warbonnet represents a specific deed of bravery. Typically, these are the most dangerous deeds associated with actions on the battlefield, such as striking the enemy with a club (as opposed to shooting him from a safe distance). Another type of brave deed that, in some tribes, could earn an eagle feather would be horse stealing. Remember, a horse stealing party must enter the country of the enemy, perhaps even sneaking into the enemy's camp at night, in order to steal horses. Then, the thieves must make safe their getaway, many times while being pursued by the "former owners". After the men returned from a successful battle or raid, meetings were held wherein the warriors recounted their exploits and vouched for deeds of comrades they had witnessed. Then, feathers would be awarded accordingly. Today, we would somewhat liken an eagle feather so earned to a military combat ribbon. The brave act itself is called a coup (pronounced "coo"), while the act of bravery is called "counting coup", and the feather associated with the deed is called a "coup feather". Thus, a warbonnet is a collection of coup feathers, and the man who owned it had, through his deeds, earned the right to have it.

And so, over time, a brave man might earn enough feathers for a warbonnet. Comanche informants in the 1930s stated that a man must earn 48 feathers (the 12 tail feathers from each of 4 eagles) before he could make a bonnet. (Because the average basic bonnet requires only around 30 feathers, they may have been speaking of one with trailers).

Somewhere along the line, the uninformed general public has come to believe that "all men who wear warbonnets are chiefs", or "only chiefs wear warbonnets". You now know that this is incorrect. So, what can be said to describe a man who wore a warbonnet? "He was a brave warrior."

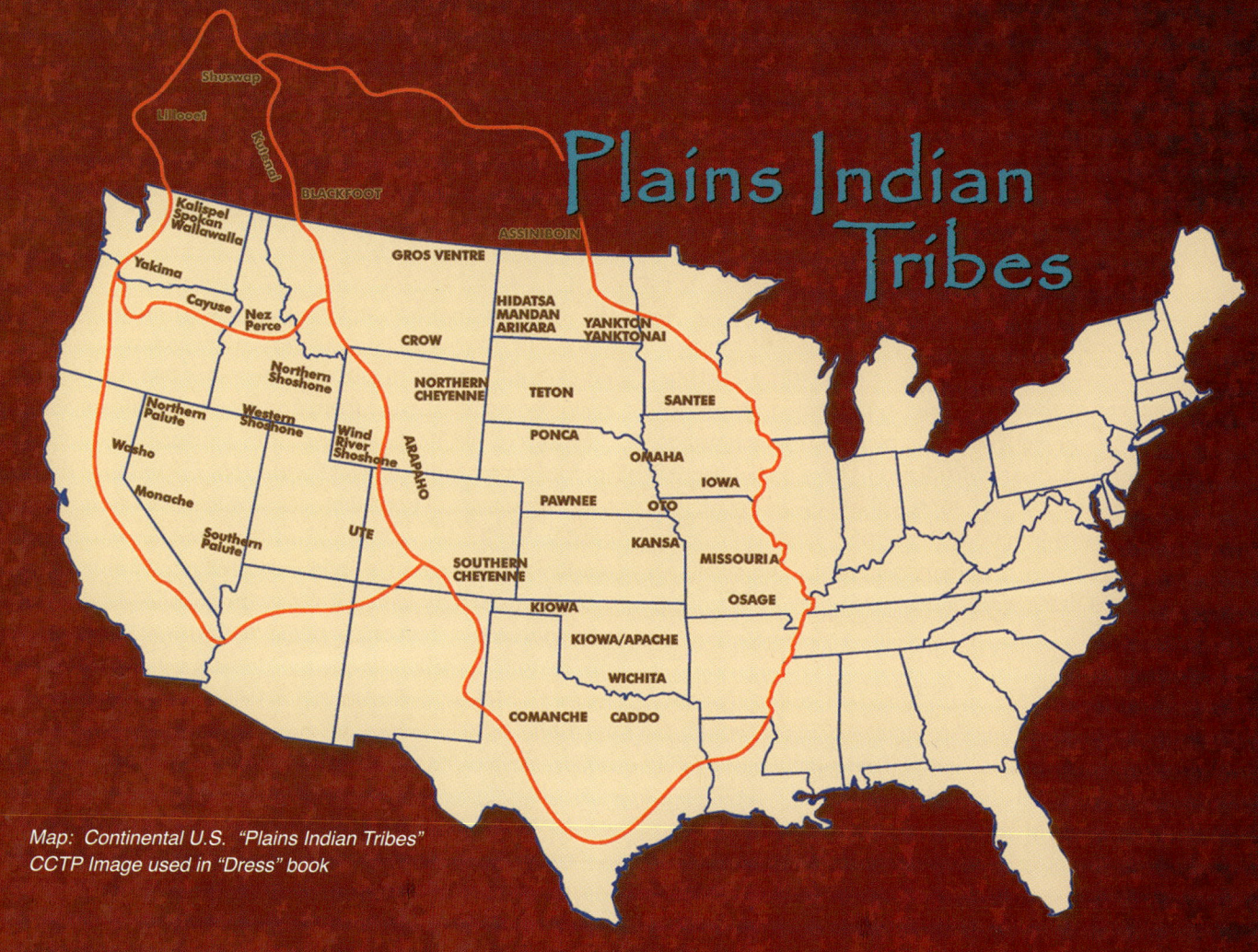

Map: Continental U.S. "Plains Indian Tribes"
CCTP Image used in "Dress" book

Map of continental US showing Plains & Plateau Tribes.

Tribes that counted coup:
Arikara, Sioux, Hidatsa, Mandan, Crow, Cheyenne, Comanches, Arapaho, Kiowas, Plains Cree, Omaha

Tribes that did not count coup:
Blackfoot and Nez Perce of the Columbia River area.

Feathers: How Were They Obtained?

"The Eagle Catcher" by E.S. Curtis
This man, probably Oglala Lakota, has taken an immature Golden Eagle.
Photo: Author's Collection

"The Eagle Catcher " by E.S. Curtis

In many Plains tribes, certain older men "had the right" to catch eagles. The literature and oral traditions tell how they would go to a remote place, dig a pit, then climb into it and loosely cover it with brush. They then reached out and placed bait on top of the brush. When an eagle landed on the bait, the man would attempt to grab its legs, then pull it into the pit and kill it. Obviously, eagle catching was a dangerous job, and, no doubt other means such as firearms were used to acquire the eagles. However, the men who had the right to perform this duty were an important source for the feathers traded and used within the tribe.

Eagle feathers were also traded between tribes, as some tribes might live in areas with greater eagle populations than their distant neighbors. For example, native stories tell us that the Crow traded feathers to the Plains Cree in exchange for hundreds of hand-carved bone elk teeth which Crow women used on their dresses.

Beinecke Rare Book and Manuscript Library, Yale University
Blood Indian, seated at a dance. Glass lantern slide by Walter McClintock, ca 1900.

The Story Behind The Warbonnet 5

What Did It Mean?

As we have shown, the feathers in the warbonnet served as a record of specific feats of bravery. However, the warbonnet of the Indian warfare period was more than a record; it was considered to have extraordinary "power". By "power", the wearer believed that the bonnet gave him strengths and abilities above that of mortal man. Indian people believe that individual feathers from a number of birds have power, with some powers/feathers being helpful and some being harmful, depending on how they are used. Eagle feathers rank among the highest power feathers and are used in various ways beyond that of warbonnets; e.g., doctoring. The most common power associated with warbonnets and the feathers they contain is protection from harm. This includes invincibility from bullets. And there were often additional "charms" attached to the bonnet to provide different kinds of powers. Various dried bird skins, animal parts, and even painted decorations representing insects or phenomena of nature (hail, whirlwinds, etc.) would impart special abilities to the wearer, such as agility to dodge an enemy's attempts to strike him, or being able to have especially keen vision, etc. Many of these decorations had their derivations in dreams experienced by the owner. As animals and birds themselves were deemed to have special powers, the wearing of the parts of one of these animals or birds was considered as a way of summoning the animals' spirits and their special powers in times of conflict. Thus, we can better appreciate how and why warbonnet adornments were individualistic and depended on the special dreams and spirit protectors for the bonnet owner.

Yellowstone County Museum, Billings, MT; 1958-1190-76

Crow men: Man on left is Big Medicine. A kingfisher is attached to his warbonnet above the browband.

And so the warbonnet and its powers could come to the aid of the wearer when he was in battle. Therefore, the warbonnet had importance far above being a spectacular article of clothing: It had spiritual and protective meanings to its owner.

However, as the reservation period progressed and the days of warfare and real warriors became memories, much of the battle-related and spiritual aspects of warbonnets have been lost. And, as the traditional importance of the bonnet diminished, its use became more common and widespread throughout tribes of North America.

How Were Warbonnets Acquired?

As we have seen, not just anyone had the right to make a bonnet. For some tribes, such as the Omaha, whenever a man accumulated sufficient feathers for a bonnet, he would call in members of his warrior society. The men would then help prepare the feathers and participate in making the bonnet. As each feather was wrapped and decorated, the warrior would relate the particular deed he had performed to earn that feather.

But warbonnets could be acquired in other ways. Often, someone else made the bonnet. For example, a man might pay a holy man or highly regarded warrior to make his bonnet for him. The warbonnet of the famous Cheyenne Roman Nose was made specifically for him by White Bull, also known as Ice. Among the Cheyenne, a suitor might give a warbonnet to his sweetheart's brother in an attempt to gain favor with the family.

Crow man with bonnet   Bud Lake photo Bud Lake & Randy Brewer Crow Collection

Crow man (possibly Chief Black Hair) with single trailer warbonnet. Fred E. Miller photo.

Beinecke Rare Book and Manuscript Library, Yale University

Night Gun, Blackfoot, at a dance. His warbonnet appears to have a pompon at the front center, and his bonnet, war shirt, and leggings are heavily decorated with ermine tubes.

Also customary with the Cheyenne, if a warrior who had not taken his warbonnet with him to battle ended up being killed, the mourning family might give the bonnet to a member of his warrior society.

The Comanche had several restrictions regarding warbonnets. If a warrior with a bonnet felt compelled to retreat during battle, he must first untie it from under his chin and throw it to the ground. Another warrior could then retrieve it for himself, and there was nothing thereafter that the original owner could do to reclaim his bonnet. Also, if a young man was anxious to go to war and boasted of his unproven bravery around the camp, the women might make him a warbonnet which he was then required to wear in his first battle. If he then acted bravely, he could keep the bonnet; if not, he forfeited it.

The Comanches, like most other tribes, had other rules regarding warbonnets and combat. For example, if a warrior fled from battle and left a comrade, then his bonnet would be confiscated. Also, if another man rode back into the battle fray to rescue a comrade, then he probably would be awarded a warbonnet.

Finally, in many tribes we see that a man's bonnet could be inherited by a son if he himself was a brave warrior.

Other Sources for Warbonnets

Throughout history, battlefield trophies have always been picked up and subsequently used again by the victors. This applied not only to weapons but shields, warbonnets, and other paraphernalia. Such a practice can account for how one tribe might have obtained bonnets from its enemies, and, subsequently the styles of the latter then influenced the future bonnet styles of the victors. This, too, may explain, in part, the use of Blackfoot-style straight up bonnets among the Nez Perce, or the fondness shared by the Blackfoot and Plateau groups for the extensive use of ermine fur.

The oral histories of many tribes tell of warbonnets being obtained by warriors on the battlefield from the slain owners. So, in addition to being made and distributed within a given tribe, some warbonnets also came through trade and warfare.

When and by Whom Were They Worn?

As described, this headdress style was foremost associated with warriors in battle. However, bonnets were also brought out during ceremonies and dances performed at camp. Early artwork and, later, photographs show bonnets being worn during dances, etc.

Typically, the warbonnet is thought of as being worn strictly by men. As far as being worn in battle, this is true (although there are numerous examples of Indian women participating in battles, fighting side by side with the men). Outside of battle, however, we have many examples of warbonnets being worn by women during ceremonies and dances.

A number of tribes permitted women to wear the bonnets of their male relatives during scalp dances and other dances honoring warriors. This holds true today, as can be seen among the Kiowa, Crow, Comanches, and other tribes – especially at Armed Forces Day or Veterans Day celebrations. The wearing of bonnets by women is a customary way in these tribes for women to honor their warrior relatives.

An interesting exception to their being worn by adults is among the Blackfoot, where The "Mini'poka" children were sometimes given warbonnets. This was a class of favored boys, usually first-born.

Beinecke Rare Book and Manuscript Library, Yale University

Large group of Blackfoot men dancers. Hand-colored glass lantern slide by Walter McClintock, ca 1900.

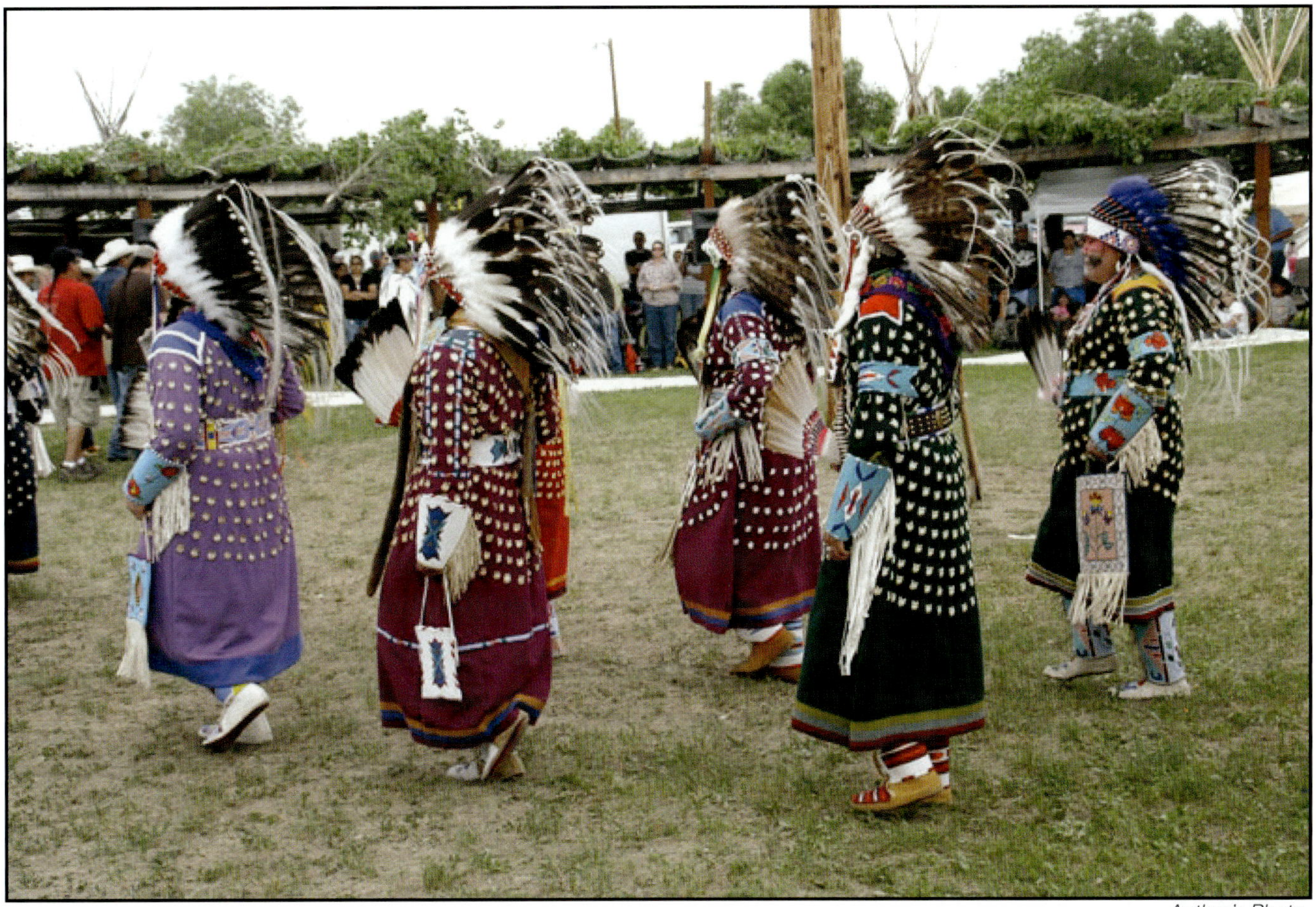

Author's Photo

***Above:** Young Crow women wear warbonnets to honor veterans during what the Crows call a "Shoshone Dance" in June, 2009.*

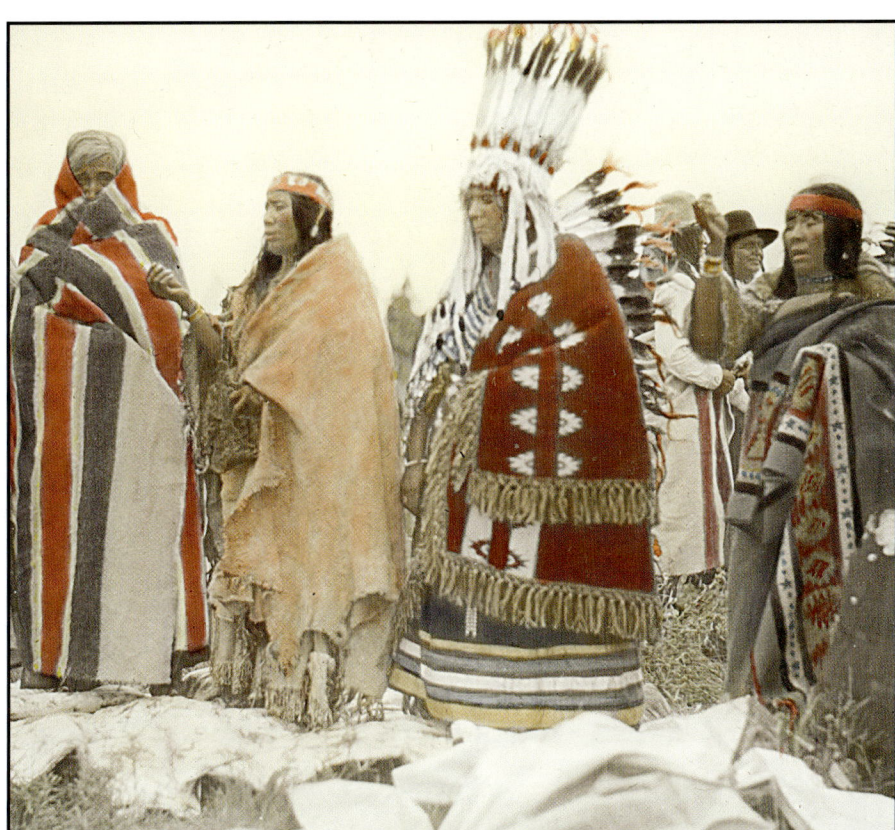

"Indians making vows and praying for the ill" is the title of this image taken of Blackfoot women, one of whom wears a Straight Up Single Trailer bonnet. Hand-colored glass lantern slide by Walter McClintock, ca 1900.

Beinecke Rare Book and Manuscript Library, Yale University

Author's Collection
These Kiowa women wear warbonnets in honor of male relatives who are Veterans. They are attending one of many dances in the early 1900s at Ft.Still, near Lawton, Oklahoma. RPPC in Author's Collection.

Storage

Typical hard containers used by Plains Indians were made from prepared rawhide – usually buffalo - and known collectively as parfleches. Both the rawhide material itself and an individual container were called parfleche. Tradition has it that warbonnets were kept in cylindrical parfleches, often in the shape of a truncated cone, which included a top and bottom. These had carrying straps so that they could handily be tied to horse gear for a war journey or when moving camp. Since the crown of a warbonnet is fairly soft, it can be folded in on itself to compact the warbonnet and thus make it easy to slip into the parfleche cylinder. Museum examples of warbonnet parfleches show them to have been painted with earth pigments, and some feature elaborately long buckskin fringe.

Bud Lake Collection
Crow rawhide parfleche cylinder.

Of course, the warbonnet crown could also be flattened, so that the bonnet could also readily be stored in a flat parfleche or large parfleche envelope.

Photo courtesy of Custer Battlefield Trading Post

Crow rawhide parfleche cylinder typically identified as a bonnet case.

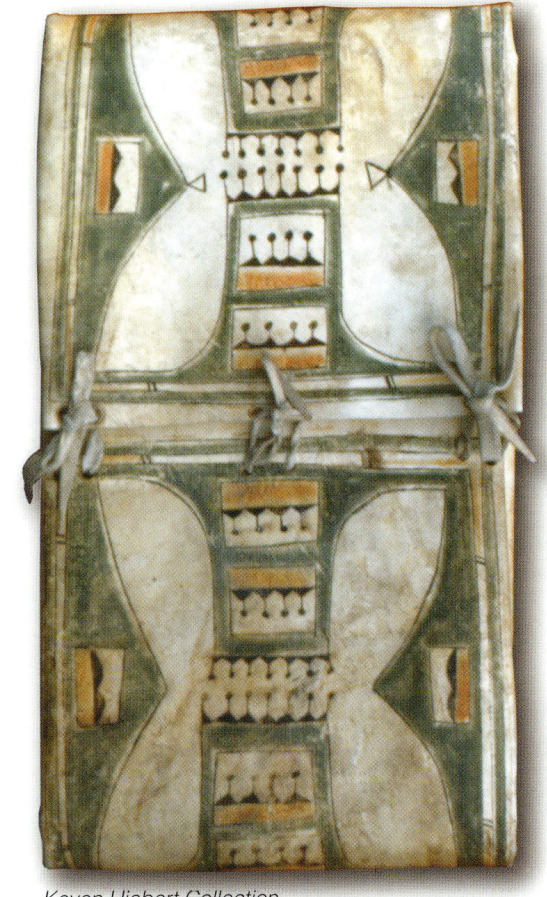

Keven Hiebert Collection

Cheyenne flat parfleche used to store a variety of items.

Yellowstone County Museum, Billings, MT; 1958-1190-73

Plains Bonnet Styles 6

Throughout the 1800s to present, warbonnets of the Plains have had several basic shapes, with variations even within these types. Oftentimes, more than one style can be observed being worn by members of the same tribe during the same time period. Though various terms have been given to these general styles, for our purposes we will use the following:

1. Flared The most popular modern shape which arranges the feathers so that, looking at the wearer from the front, the bonnet fans out symmetrically around his head. Typically found on Sioux and Crow warbonnets (but other tribes as well).
(Fig. 1a, 1b, 1c, and 1d)

Fig. 1a Left Photo

Plenty Coups (1848 – 1932), Crow Chief. Photo by Wm. Wildschut. Plenty Coups' warbonnet has a brow band with Crow geometric designs, at each end of which is attached a small carved horn. Whole ermine skins and a ribbon were used for side drops.

Fig. 1b Right Photo

Portrait of Yankton Dakota Man. The feathers in his trailer bonnet are widely spaced, exaggerating the overall size of this Flared Style.

Yankton man
Wisconsin Historical Society, 27831

Buffalo Bill Historical Center, Cody, Wyoming, U.S.A.; Gift of J.W. Duke Wellington, NA.203.334

Fig. 1c

Warbonnet collected from the Ft. Belknap Reservation, ca. 1920. Immature golden eagle feathers are laced to a felt crown. The tips have yellow horsehair and red tip fluffs.

Fig. 1d

Back of the Ft. Belknap bonnet showing the crown adorned with small eagle tertiary feathers. Note that there is no Major Plume.

Buffalo Bill Historical Center, Cody, Wyoming, U.S.A.; Gift of J.W. Duke Wellington, NA.203.334

2. Swept Back Looking at the wearer head-on, only the front feathers are visualized, while the remainder fall back on either side. Seen in Cheyenne, Comanche, and Kiowa bonnets of the Indian Wars Period, as well as other tribes. (Fig. 2a, 2b, and 2c)

Denver Public Library, Western History Collection

Fig. 2a *Chief Timbo, Comanche, a friend of Quanah Parker's. The Swept Back Trailer Bonnet he wears may have belonged to Quanah. The base of each feather is beaded. This photo includes many examples of a Comanche man's dress accoutrements of the late 1800s – early 1900s. Timbo holds a fully-beaded lance, similar to the one carried by Quanah in Fig. 7-45.*

Fig. 2b

Blackfeet bonnet ca. 1945-1955 of immature golden eagle feathers. This example has beaded rosettes and ermine tube side drops. The small base plumes are dyed blue. Note spiral wraps of white tape around the red wool quill wraps.

Buffalo Bill Historical Center, Cody, Wyoming, U.S.A.; Presented in 1955 to John M. Cooper (1899-1982) by Blackfeet Tribal Leaders. Donated in his memory by his son, Jack., NA.205.82

Fig. 2c

Warbonnet of mature golden eagle tail feathers, maker unknown. Brow band has Sioux style design beaded in lane stitch. Side drops are ribbons and ermine tubes. Tip decorations include orange tip fluffs, ermine fur spots, and white horsehair.

Courtesy of the Wagner Museum, Germany.

3. Stand Out The feathers are a more tightly strung cluster than the Flared bonnet, yet they do not fall on the wearer's neck or shoulders. Seen in many historic photos as being worn by men of several tribes. **(Fig. 3a, 3b, and 3c)**

Denver Public Library, Western History Collection

Fig. 3a *Shoshone men at Ft. Hall, ID, early 1900s. Man at left has Stand Out style of bonnet while man at right wears a Flared syle.*

Fig. 3b
Below: Northern Plains bonnet ca. 1930 of mature golden eagle tail feathers laced to a felt hat crown. The brow band is loom beaded. Feather bases are wrapped with red cloth.

Buffalo Bill Historical Center, Cody, Wyoming, U.S.A.; Dr. Robert L. Anderson Collection, NA.205.64

Yellowstone County Museum, Billings, MT; 1958-1190-41

Fig. 3c
Above: White Swan (1851-1904), Crow, one of Custer's Scouts, with feathered lance.
Fred E. Miller photo.

4. Straight Up All the feathers are gathered closely and stand up so as to form a "feather tube". Commonly associated with the Blackfeet but also used by some other Plateau tribes. **(Fig. 4a, 4b, and 4c)**

Beinecke Rare Book and Manuscript Library, Yale University

Fig. 4a *In this hand-colored lantern slide by Wm. McClintock of a Blackfoot in his ceremonial regalia ca. 1900, the man wears a Straight Up bonnet with a center pompon of red rooster hackles. Porcupine quill-wrapped rawhide strips are attached to the main quill of each feather. Note the prolific use of ermine to decorate his headgear and war shirt.*

Fig. 4b

Left: Stand Up bonnet, Blackfeet, ca. 1880. This splendid example is finely decorated with a red trade cloth brow band trimmed with brass buttons, ermine fur "fringes", and bells; immature golden eagle tail feathers adorned with porcupine quilled rawhide strips and tip decorations of rooster hackles and horsehair; and a large number of ermine tubes suspended from the open crowned head band.

Buffalo Bill Historical Center, Cody, Wyoming, U.S.A.; Chandler-Pohrt Collection, Gift of Mr. and Mrs. Richard A. Pohrt, Sr., NA.203.357

Fig. 4c

Right: Piegan (Blackfeet) man with Straight Up bonnet made from mature golden eagle tail feathers. His feathered staff is similarly decorated.

Piegan with Straight Up Bonnet E.S. Curtis

5. Trailer Bonnets: At the back of the crown of a standard bonnet, a cloth or leather panel was attached that extended down several feet. Down the trailer was either a Single or Double row of eagle feathers, giving rise to the popular designations of Single Trailer or Double Trailer Warbonnet respectively. **(Fig. 5a, 5b, and 5c)**

Yellowstone County Museum, Billings, MT; 1958-1190-54

Fig. 5a

Left: Sioux Double Trailer Warbonnet, ca. 1920-30. Thirty immature golden eagle tail feathers are laced to a buckskin skull cap. The brow band has lane stitched beadwork in a Sioux design, at the ends of which are beaded rosettes. A more modern look is achieved with the use of pink fluffs and tip plumes. There are a total of 72 tail feathers on the split-tailed trailer which is made of buckskin. Partly visible on the lower back of the edge-beaded trailer are painted images of turtles, pipes, and geometric designs.

Fig. 5b

Above: Plain Owl (1861-1921), Crow, with sacred Tobacco Ceremony ritual bird-head staff. He wears a single trailer warbonnet that extends all the way to the ground. Fred E. Miller photo.

Buffalo Bill Historical Center, Cody, Wyoming, U.S.A.; The Catherine Bradford Collection, Gift of The Coe Foundation, NA.205.14a/b

Fig. 5c

Crow man with Single Trailer Bonnet of immature golden eagle tail feathers. The trailer's extra length gives the owner an even more striking appearance as he rides. These long trailers are especially popular with Indians who ride in parades. Midway down the trailer, and again about 2 feet from the bottom, single eagle "breath plumes" are attached as trailer ornaments.

Bud Lake & Randy Brewer Crow Collection

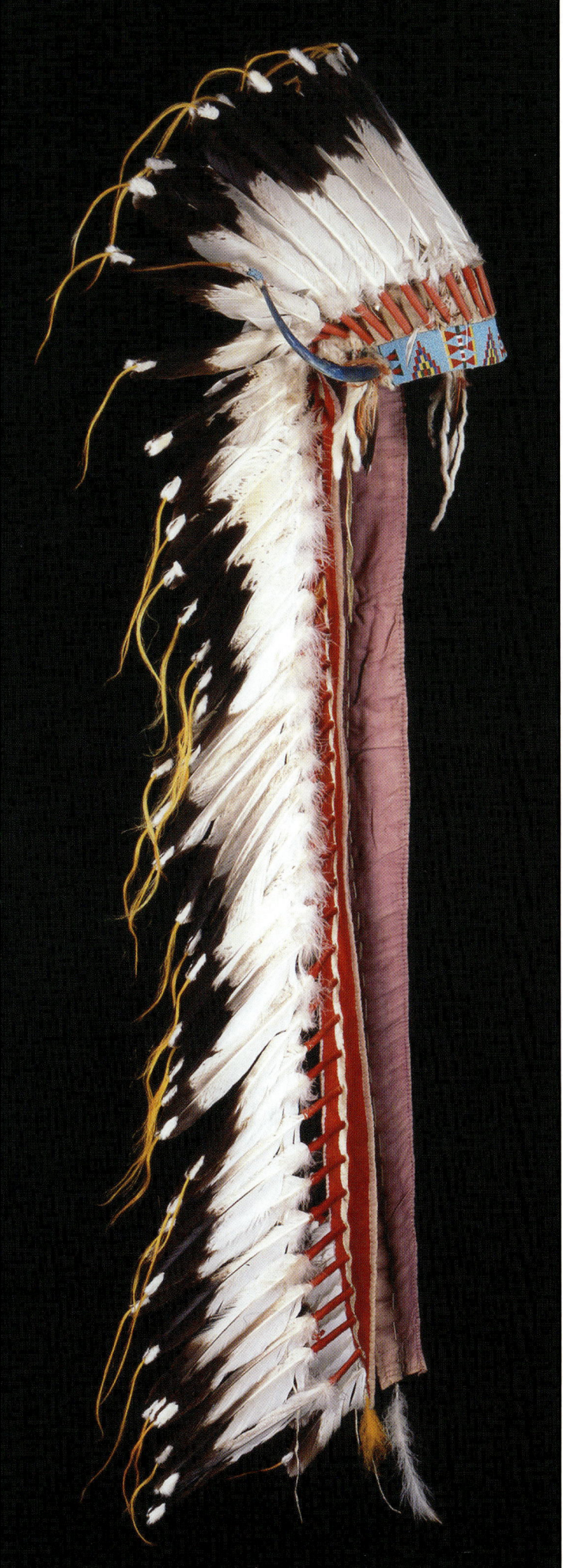

6. Horned Bonnet

A variation on the above styles. Sometimes a pair of small horns (usually buffalo) was attached on either side of the crown at the ends of the brow band. These horns adorned feathered warbonnets made in the typical styles, as well as many headdress examples made without a feather crown. **(Fig. 6-1)**

MORE ABOUT BONNET STYLES

Flared Bonnet

The oldest specimen of this familiar style was collected in 1838. This style was the one most commonly copied by other tribes who adopted the warbonnet into their culture in the late 1800s-early 1900s. In fact, some Indians today whose tribes have long had warbonnets will unwittingly insist on having the flared style when, in reality, the traditional style for their tribe is the Swept Back version.

Swept Back Bonnet

This bonnet was first documented on the Plains in the early 19th century, when, in 1811, Henry Brakenridge reported of the Arikara that "Some were dressed in their most gaudy stile, with the cincture of feathers, and their ornaments of the head made of plumes, fitted round a kind of crown." This is the first known mention of a crown instead of a band, and it is significantly different in construction and appearance than the flared and stand-up styles. This swept back bonnet is also documented as being known to the Pawnee and the Potawatomi in 1820-23. **(See Page 10 Petalesharro, Pawnee ca. 1822)**

The Blackfoot and Nez Perce seem to have adopted this shape at a later date, possibly due to trade resulting from increased communication between tribes.

Fig. 6-1

Shoshone Double Trailer Horned Bonnet, ca. 1915. Buffalo horns were split and carved down, then attached to the crown at each end of the brow band which is beaded in applique style. The bottoms of the 86 immature golden eagle feathers are wrapped with red yarn, rather than red wool. This split trailer fabric style allows the ends to fall on either side of a horse's rump.

Buffalo Bill Historical Center, Cody, Wyoming, U.S.A.;
Adolf Spohr Collection, Gift of Larry Sheerin, NA.205.3

The swept back style was observed among the Kiowa on the Southern Plains but was probably carried with them when they left the Black Hills area in the late 1700s. Their allies, the Comanches, also adopted this bonnet shape.

Stand Out

Though this style might be considered by some as a variation of the Swept Back style, historic photos show that it was so commonplace as to warrant its own designation. These bonnets were strung tightly enough with the secondary lace so that they did not flare nor fall back narrowly like the Swept Back style. As you can see, the back feathers do not touch the wearer's back. This style was favored by a number of tribes. It undoubtedly was more aerodynamic than the Flared or Swept Back styles, a characteristic which undoubtedly made it more comfortable to wear on the wind-swept Plains.

Straight Up Bonnet

The Blackfoot Indians are of the Algonquian linguistic stock, and their unique style of warbonnet may be similar to those of the ancestral migrants from the New England area. Upon arriving on the Plains, they found different birds, such as eagles, with feathers uniquely suited for use in what we have come to know as the familiar style bonnet. From this, we can speculate that the development of the Blackfoot "stand-up" bonnet had its beginnings in the east. This vertically styled bonnet was constructed using a rawhide band with 18-30 eagle tail feathers attached in a rigid manner, so as to afford little movement to the feathers. From the earliest times, only acknowledged leaders could wear it, including a society of older men known as the Bulls. Today, it is still considered sacred, with very few men having the right to wear it.

This type of construction seemed prevalent in the Upper Missouri River area at least as early as 1830, as evidenced by the headdress of Chief Mato-tope, Mandan, which was collected at that time by Maximilian, Prince of Wied. Constructed from twenty-seven golden eagle tail feathers decorated with short red hackles, quill-wrapped leather strips in yellow, white, and brown; and mounted on a base covered with red cloth, this fine early example of a stand-up bonnet resides in the collection of the Linden-Museum in Stuttgart, Germany. The Plains Cree had a similar headdress but used a shorter feather (12" – 13"), and this may also have been influenced by their eastern neighbors. The Nez Perce and Flatheads are other Transmontanes tribe known to have used the stand-up bonnet.

Trailer Bonnets

Among tribes that wore the basic crown-of-feathers warbonnet can be seen examples of Trailer Bonnets. "Trailer" refers to a panel of cloth that extends several feet off the back of the bonnet crown. Attached to the cloth would be either a single or double row of eagle feathers. The Single Trailer bonnet had one feather row attached to the center of the panel, while the Double Trailer had two feather rows, each of which extended down either side of the panel. Paintings made by Catlin on his trip to the Plains (1832-37) document trailer bonnets among several tribes.

Different Styles, Same Tribe

As you study historic photos, you will sometimes see more than one bonnet style being worn by men of the same tribe, such as the Flared and Swept Back bonnet worn by these Sioux man.

Fig. 6-2

A group of Sioux leaders, including from left: No Neck, Yankton Charlie, Flat Iron, Spotted Tail, and Standing Bear. These men are gathered in a camp for Buffalo Bill's Wild West Show at Ambrose Park in Brooklyn, NY. (1894?) No Neck wears a Flared style of bonnet, and Standing Bear's is of the Stand Out style.

Buffalo Bill Historical Center, Cody, Wyoming, U.S.A.; NA.205.65

38 Northern Plains war bonnet. This bonnet has several features associated with "typical" 20th century examples, notably the many decorative extras. The crown is made from an old felt hat. Beaded rosettes are attached at each end of the brow band, and whole skin ermines were used as side drops. Two different thread bands (faded green and yellow yarn) were used on the firecrackers. Ermine fur spots have been applied to the feather quills, both near the quill end and at the tip. (The tip spots are dyed red.) Interestingly, the quill of the Major Plume was split, and the two decorated ends are visible in the right of the photo.

Materials and Construction Basics 7

These are the basic components of the typical Plains warbonnet:

- Crown
- Feathers
- Feather Loops
- "Firecrackers" (red wool wraps at bottoms of feathers.)
- Base Plumes
- Lacing
- Brow Band
- Rosettes
- Side Drops
- Feather Tip Decorations
- Crown decorations (Include completely covering the crown with wool or calico cloth, etc.)
- Major Plume
- Trailer (optional)

Following is a brief discussion of each. Again, you are encouraged to do more research to help you decide on specifics for designing your own warbonnet.

Crown

The primary characteristic of material for making a crown is that it should be somewhat stiff. The entire finished shape of the warbonnet depends on the quality of the crown, such that it will hold the feathers in the desired positions when worn.

Many crowns were made of tanned leather. Crown leather should be somewhat thick and non-stretchy. Today, you may consider tanned cowhide, elk, or moderately thick moose. Deer skin generally is too soft and will tend to stretch. However, whatever leather or material you use should be soft enough to be comfortable when worn, but it also must have some body to it.

Indians found early on that the felt hats of the white man had enough body to be appropriate for a bonnet crown, and many old specimens were made this way. If you buy a modern felt hat or felt crown designed for the purpose, be sure it is not flimsy.

Your first instinct may be to make a crown from four identically shaped leather pieces. However, there are also examples of two and three piece crowns. Before you begin to make your cap or even cut a hat or felt crown to size, you should make a fabric pattern. Look at old photos to see how warbonnets were worn. Some of the Indians wore them with the front brim high on the forehead, while others wore them pulled lower in front. How you choose to wear yours will also contribute to how the bonnet feathers lay back.

Although an acceptable bonnet may be made from a symmetrical bowl-shaped crown, the Swept Back style – and even some Flared Style – crowns are made so that the back is longer than the front. If you make your crown from a hat with brim, then include a short bill-like extension toward the back when you cut it out. The same shape must be incorporated when making a leather crown from scratch for this bonnet style.

Feathers

In the old days, tail feathers from immature golden eagles were the predominant warbonnet feathers. These are the beautiful "black and whites" witnessed in so many photos. **(Fig. 7-1)**

Fig. 7-1

Complete 12 feather tail set from immature golden eagle.

We also have examples where eagle secondary wing feathers were incorporated on the back half or one-third of the bonnet, and, occasionally, you will find warbonnets made completely from eagle secondary wing feathers (becoming more common and accepted in post-reservation times). **(Fig. 7-2)**

Fig. 7-2

Secondary wing feathers from right wing of immature golden eagle.

Mature golden eagle tail feathers were an option, **(Fig. 7-3)** and sometimes mature or immature bald eagle tail feathers were used. **(Fig. 7-4)**

Fig. 7-3

Complete 12 feather tail set from mature golden eagle.

Buffalo Bill Historical Center, Cody, Wyoming, U.S.A.; Gift of Hope Williams Read in memory of Barry Williams, NA.205.94

Fig. 7-4

Northern Plains bonnet of Immature Bald Eagle Tail Feathers. Brow band is ermine fur "fringe" in lieu of a beaded strip, at the ends of which is a shell button "rosette". Crown made from a felt hat.

There also are rare instances of warbonnets made from eagle wing primary feathers ("spikes"), but these are the exception. **(Fig. 7-5)**

Buffalo Bill Historical Center, Cody, Wyoming, U.S.A.;
Gift of Hon. and Mrs. William Henry Harrison, NA.205.10

Fig. 7-5
Single Trailer war bonnet made completely of mature golden eagle primary wing spikes. Northern Plains. Crown is commercial leather, and the trailer is red trade cloth. Hawk feather drops are attached at the end of the brow band beaded in lane stitch.

Warbonnet by Mike Tucker.

Fig. 7-6
This beautiful bonnet was made by Mike Tucker, using select hand-painted imitation eagle feathers created from turkey wing feathers.

Because of the length and width of real eagle feathers, twenty four to thirty or so feathers could make a full, handsome bonnet. (Some historic examples have as few as twenty.) However, because of federal migratory bird laws, genuine eagle feathers are no longer available to a non-Indian person in the United States. As a substitute, we must use imitation eagle feathers fashioned from processed turkey wing feathers. **(Fig. 7-6)**

However, these feathers are neither the size nor shape of real eagle feathers, and so we make modifications to achieve end results similar to the old bonnets. This requires using more feathers, adding extensions, and reshaping and straightening the naturally curved turkey wing feathers so that they resemble handsome eagle tail feathers.

Imitation eagle feathers can either be purchased or made. The store-bought versions range from the inexpensive bleached white/black tipped feathers to well-done hand painted products. **(Fig. 7-7)**

Fig. 7-7

A group of hand-painted imitation eagle tail feathers, all lefts.

The hand-painted feathers have been selected for quality out of large batches of feathers, straightened, hand trimmed to eagle feather shapes, and then skillfully painted with characteristic eagle feather markings. However, for the ambitious craftsman, there now are books available so you can learn to make your own feathers to resemble those of eagles and other migratory birds. The trick is to be able to acquire a sufficient number of bleached white turkey wing feathers from which to select a quality warbonnet set.

Today, because turkey feathers are narrow, approximately 36 imitation eagle feathers are required to make a warbonnet.

Feather Loops

An often unappreciated component of a good warbonnet is the leather loop applied to the bottom of each feather which facilitates lacing the feathers to the crown. A poor-looking bonnet will have flimsy soft leather loops with the loop diameter being so large that the feather wobbles and falls far back when the bonnet is worn.

Indians used thin rawhide for their loops. These were inflexible, which meant that the bottoms of the feathers, once laced to the crown, would stay in position.

The result was that the front of the warbonnet fairly well maintained its upright shape, even on a windy day. If the loops themselves are any bigger than necessary for the lace to pass through, then, again, the feathers will not lay properly.

Typical craft instructions today tell the maker to tie or glue the leather loop to the end of the feather quill. However, Indians had another, even more secure attachment method. Examination of a number of old bonnets reveals that the quill end of the feather was smashed flat. Then the rawhide strip was looped around it, and the strip was sinew sewn to the quill, with the stitches passing front to back, back to front. **(Fig. 7-8)** This method ensured that the loop was permanently attached to the feather.

Photographer unknown

Fig. 7-8

Detail of feather attached with a rawhide loop to a historic war shirt. Loop was sewn and wrapped to quill using sinew.

Whichever attachment method you choose, be sure to use rawhide or thin, very stiff leather for the loop material.

Historical Note: Because real eagle feathers are relatively long, a number of old examples demonstrate no leather/rawhide loop at all. Rather, the end of the quill was cut back, then folded into itself to create a self-loop. **(Fig. 7-9)**

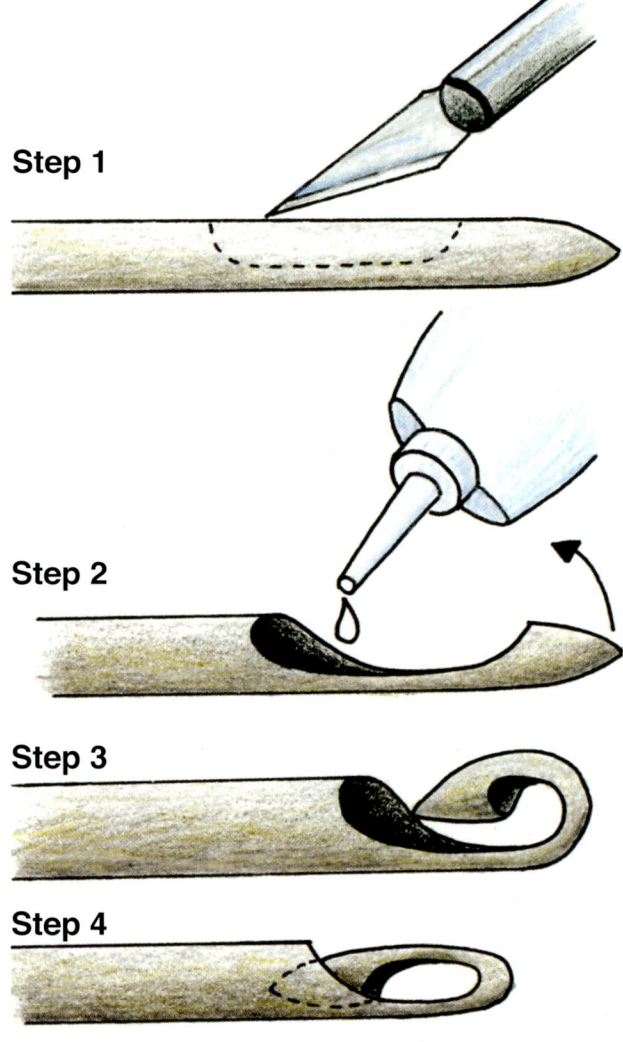

Step 1

Step 2

Step 3

Step 4

Fig. 7-9:
Steps to making a self-loop in feather quill. Cut out section near quill end, apply glue inside upper opening, then fold quill tip and insert it into upper quill.

"Firecrackers"

A term casually applied by today's craftsmen in reference to the red fabric wrap on the bottoms of bonnet feathers is "firecracker", for obvious reasons. Almost universally, red trade wool was used for feather wraps. However, there are also old examples of other colors of wool, such as dark blue and green, as well as plain smoked buckskin. Some modern bonnets evince artistic expression through the use of almost any other primary color, such as yellow, hot pink, etc. **(Fig. 7-10)** An inexpensive substitute for red wool is red felt. However, this tends to fray and fade badly over time.

Buffalo Bill Historical Center, Cody, Wyoming, U.S.A.; Irving H. "Larry" Larom Collection, NA.205.63

Fig. 7-10:
Northern Plains War Bonnet, ca. 1905. Made with immature golden eagle tail feathers attached to a felt hat crown. Yellow cloth covers the base of each feather, secured with thread wraps. Feather tips have green dyed horsehair. Side drops are whole ermine hides and strips of red saved list trade cloth. The brow band is lane stitched and edge beaded.

As you examine old photos, you will see that, once the red wool is applied, it may or not have added wrappings of colored thread. There are many old bonnets with no thread wraps, while the "standard" was to have a small band of thread at the top and bottom of each "firecracker". You will even see three and four thread wraps per feather on some bonnets. And an especially attractive variation seen on many Crow and other bonnets is a spiral thread wrap. **(See Fig. 2b, Chapter 6.)**

The red wool piece was often stitched up the back, which allowed for a uniform, straight appearance. However, stitching became less necessary when three or four thread wraps were applied, and so some bonnets with thread wraps have no additional sewing.

Thread color was typically white, although yellow or yellow-gold give an added artistic touch. Upon close examination, an interesting and uncommon variation for colored bands was to use strips of dried eagle pericardium instead of thread. The pericardium is the "sac" that surrounds the heart. When dried, this tissue is white, thin, and stiff. It can be cut into strips and attached at either end of the firecracker, like the placement of thread bands. **(Fig. 7-11)**

Specimen and photo courtesy of Billy Maxwell.

Fig. 7-11

Pericardium strip wrapped on trade wool firecracker. This example and photo courtesy of Billy Maxwell.

Base Plumes

The typical "Hollywood bonnet" has a profusion of plumes (also called fluffies) tied at the base of each feather, the ends of which are also covered by the red wool. Some bonnets have such a thick layer of base plumes that you can see but little of the eagle feathers. However, as you review old photos, you will find that such was not the case "back in the day".

Warbonnets did not all have base plumes. **(See Fig. 3-b, Chapter 6.)** Those that did often had a small number, and base plumes were not always used on the back of each feather. In those times, the so-called breath plumes from the underside base of the eagle's tail were used. Today, we use turkey plumes. And today, as then, these base plumes can be of different colors.

Your research will also reveal that other kinds of feathers can be used in addition to or instead of fluffies. Cheyenne and Sioux bonnets, for example, would sometimes incorporate short wing coverlet feathers which were white with black tips, resembling miniature tail feathers. **(See Fig. 6-2 of Sioux men, Ch. 5)** Another variation would be the use of dyed rooster hackles either in addition to or instead of base plumes.

Lacing

The thong used to lace the prepared feathers to the bonnet crown was typically of leather. Soft leather is fine; just make sure it is of sufficient diameter to fill the holes of the feather loops. Another consideration to lacing is that the lace holes cut in the bonnet crown should not be overly large, just long enough to admit the leather lace.

Tip: To help the feathers maintain an upright position, the feathers across the front should be laced tightly. As you lace toward the back of the bonnet, you should relax the tension on the lace so that the feathers can lie properly and have movement.

Brow Band

The photographic record shows that not all bonnets had a beaded brow band. **(Fig. 7-12)** Yet, many did and, regardless of the tribe, the most common bead design element was a series of tipis/mountains. **(Fig. 7-13)** Traditionally, brow bands were beaded in lazy stitch or applique **(Fig. 7-14)** or, alternatively, completely quilled. **(See Cover Photo)** The technique used depended on the tribe, so this is another detail worthy of scrutiny when researching bonnet construction. The loom beaded brow band did not gain popularity until the 1900s, and now it is the most commonly used beading technique, regardless of tribal style.

Denver Public Library, Western History Collection

Fig. 7-12

Crow Eagle, Dakota ca. 1880. Photo by D.F. Barry. In this studio portrait, Crow Eagle wears a war bonnet of immature golden eagle feathers mounted to a commercial hat crown. It is fairly unadorned, with no brow band, side drops, or base plumes. Barely visible are spiral thread wraps on the "firecrackers", and chin ties secure the bonnet to his head.

Author's Photo. Courtesy of Oklahoma History Museum.

Fig. 7-13

Southern Cheyenne lane beaded brow band. The bottom edge is even with the edge of the crown, as evidenced from the whip stitching along the bottom of the band. Variations of the simple tipi design were commonly used on Cheyenne war bonnet brow bands.

Author's Photo. Courtesy Ft. Sill Museum, Ft. Sill, Oklahoma

Fig. 7-14

Brow band beaded using applique' technique. This war bonnet belonged to I-See-o, Kiowa, who later scouted for the military. Applique' beadwork was commonly done by the Kiowas, in addition to other beading techniques.

Much individuality was demonstrated in this area of bonnet construction. Instead of or in addition to a beaded or quilled brow band strip, you will see rows of hawk bells, ermine strips, brass shoe buttons, gilt braid, brass sequins, etc. **(Fig. 7-15 & Fig. 7-16)**

Bud Lake & Randy Brewer Crow Collection

Fig. 7-15

Hoop On The Forehead, Crow, ca. 1908, served as a scout for several U.S. military commanders in the Indian Wars of the 1870s. A row of brass hawk bells is mounted above the beaded brow band of his warbonnet, along with several more bells on the bottom center of the band.

Denver Public Library, Western History Collection

Fig. 7-16

American Horse, Lakota. Photo by D.F. Barry, probably in the 1880s. A piece of metallic fringe covers the beaded brow band on American Horse's war bonnet. Along the top of the fringe is a row of small round objects which may be small brass tacks or shoe buttons. Small mirrors are mounted at the ends of the brow band.

Denver Public Library, Western History Collection

Fig. 7-17

Good Horse, Lakota. The bottom edge of his brow band extends below the bottom edge of the crown. The feather tips have horse hair tassels, the lower ends of which appear to be covered with a white paste. His magnificent otter "breastplate" is decorated with quillwork, mirrors, and a commercial metal badge. Photo by D.F. Barry, probably in the 1880s.

As for the beaded brow bands, most are 1" – 1 ¾" wide, consisting of 2, 3, or more rows of lane stitch, although there are many examples of appliqué beadwork on brow bands (depending on the tribe). The beadwork is done on a separate piece of leather, and its length can run from approximately 10" to as much as half the circumference of the crown. (Most modern brow bands are approximately 10".) When looking at photos, note the placement of the brow band on various crowns. They most often are attached so that the bottom of the brow band is in line with the bottom edge of the crown. Some examples show the beaded strip sewn so that its lower half extends below the edge of the crown. **(Fig. 7-17)**

Modern bonnets that use loom beaded strips almost always have the bead strip sewn directly to the crown (instead of a separate piece of leather) with the lower edge of the strip aligned with that of the crown.

Rosettes

The placement of a pair of matching beaded rosettes, one at each end of the brow band, is mostly a modern convention. Hardly any pre-1900 Plains bonnet had beaded rosettes, mirrors, shell discs, or quilled wheels attached at brow band ends. Those with these kinds of decorations have the rosette positioned slightly overlapping the very end of the brow band. **(Fig. 7-18)**

Author's Photo. Courtesy of Oklahoma History Museum.

Fig. 7-18
Detail of a Southern Cheyenne War Bonnet. A simple rosette beaded in applique style with edge beading slightly overlaps the end of the lane stitched brow band. Metal sequins are individually sewn beneath the brow band itself.

Side Drops

Instead of rosettes, older bonnets typically only had some kind of "drops" that were sewn to the crown beginning where the brow band ended. These drops were most often ribbons, ermine (complete hides, fur strips, or ermine tubes), or short or medium-length feathers or breath plumes. The drops might be attached to only the first 2"-3" just back of the brow band, or they might be sewn along the entire crown edge, going all around the back to the other side. Typically, two or more kinds of drops might be attached. **(Fig. 7-19) Also see cover photo and Figures 5a & 7-10.**

Fig. 7-19:
Crow man wearing trailer bonnet. Side drops at the end of the brow band are of several materials, including ribbons, ermine tubes, and feathers of at least two different kinds of birds.

Yellowstone County Museum, Billings, MT: 1958-1190-133

Ermine Drops

Ermine side drops consist of two types: Complete skins and ermine tubes. **(Fig. 7-20 & Fig. 7-21)** Many times these terminate at the top with a red wool wrap, like those at the base of each bonnet feather. When complete skins are used, they most often are case skinned furs. "Case skinning" refers to leaving the hide intact as it is removed from the carcass, rather like an open-ended sock. It is peeled off in one piece without first having cut the hide down the midline of the belly. Of course, this type of drop can be made by taking a complete hide that was split up the belly, sewing it up inside out, then turning it right side out and attaching a leather tie and "firecracker". Complete skins are usually seen on the more modern bonnets, as they take considerably less time to make than ermine tubes.

Portrait of Yumyekalimpt   Wisconsin Historical Society, 28008

Fig. 7-20
Left: Plenty Coups, Crow Chief. Whole, case-skinned ermine hides were used for side drops on Plenty Coups' bonnet..

Fig. 7-21
Above: Yumyekalimpt (aka Jesse Stevens), Nez Perce/Shahaptian, early 1900s. His bonnet has side drops of several ermine tubes at each end of the brow band. Photo by De Lancey Gill.

Yellowstone County Museum, Billings, MT; 1958-1190-205

Horned Bonnets

There are some examples where a warrior incorporated a pair of buffalo horns on a typical style warbonnet. These were placed at each end of the brow band where you would normally consider sewing a rosette. Usually these were not the entire horn but a horn-shaped piece resulting from reducing in size a full-sized horn, perhaps by splitting it or otherwise shaving it down. Holes were drilled in the bottom of these horn pieces so that they could be laced or sewn to the crown. **(Fig. 7-22)** Of course, such a powerful symbol as buffalo horns undoubtedly would have been part of the man's personal medicine or dream associated with the warbonnet.

Feather Tip Decorations

A striking feature of many a warbonnet is the way spots, fluffs, and/or horsehair has been added to the tip of each feather. **(Fig. 7-23a & Fig. 7-23b)** However, whether or not to decorate the tips – and how – was individualistic. Many old bonnets have no tip decorations whatsoever.

Bonnet and Photo by Dr. Bill Holm

Fig. 7-22
This beautiful reproduction war bonnet was made by the distinguished artist, Dr. Bill Holm. The horns are buffalo horns, split and reduced by carving and polishing. On each horn tip is a small piece of ermine fur and tassel of yellow horsehair. Dr. Holm also made the figure on which the war bonnet is mounted.

Photo by Joe Rosenthal

Fig. 7-23a
Round white spots, fluffs, and horsehair adorn the tips of hand-painted imitation eagle feathers in this bonnet by Joe Rosenthal who also provided the photo.

Author's Photo. Courtesy of Oklahoma History Museum.

Fig. 7-23b

Detail of tip decorations of wing spikes used in trailer of a Cheyenne bonnet.

It is easier to dye an entire tail than to dye bunches of commercial hair. (Of course, you also can buy dyed hair, but you may want a different shade than what is readily available.) Rit (TM) dye is a good dye for horsehair, and mixing scarlet and some yellow or yellow-gold will allow you to achieve the old red-orange color found on many bonnets. Be sure to set the dye with vinegar per Rit's instructions, then thoroughly rinse the hair until the water is clear.

It is important to mention that it is easy to put too much weight on the end of bonnet feathers. Remember, turkey feathers are not as stout as eagle feathers, and the turkey quill at the tip is especially thin. Be sure and trim the ends of your turkey feathers per the instructions and cut them down to where the quill is not so flimsy that it will break with the weight of tip decorations.

Whatever type of hair you use, the bunches can be glued on with many types of glue, including white craft glue.

Although some bonnets had no decoration over the glued ends of the hair bunches, many did. One option was to apply a white paste-like substance over the hair bunch in either a spot or rectangular pattern. This paste could be made from glue and white clay (especially if the clay is micaceous gypsum). A modern substitute might be chalk or plaster of Paris mixed with glue. You will notice that the paste on old bonnets was dabbed on, usually without great precision. **(Fig. 7-24)**

The most common tip decoration on old bonnets was to glue on individual bunches of horsehair. Mane hair is the first choice, as it seems to move better than the coarser tail hair. Some bonnets used cow's tail hair. As you will see in photographs, the hair tips are often wavy. Cow tail hair is naturally wavy, but waves can be put into horsehair. An efficient way to do this is as follows: Prepare all the feathers, including the addition of hair bunches to the tips. Then, braid all of the hair together into a single braid, spritz the braid with hot water, then let it dry. When the dried braid is undone, you'll have wavy horsehair.

Hair collected from an entire tail will have a natural taper to the end of each hair. So, if you can get whole dried horse or cow tails, this will result in a more pleasing effect than the commercial horsehair which has both ends sheared off. Also, many times the feather tip hair was dyed. Red and yellow were popular choices, with the Cheyennes showing a penchant for yellow. Among the Omaha, each eagle feather stood for an enemy man, and a dyed-red hair tip represented the man's scalp lock. Only a man who had taken the scalp of an enemy could put tips of red hair on his feathers.

Author's Photo. Courtesy of Oklahoma History Museum.

Fig. 7-24

Gypsum was dabbed on these feather tips over the glued ends of the horsehair tassels.

Instead of the white paste, another choice was to glue some kind of material over the glued area. This material took several forms, most commonly pieces of ermine skin, buckskin, eagle pericardium, or even more modern materials such as rabbit fur or white surgical tape. The shape of these "spots" can be round, rectangular, diamond-shaped, etc. **(Fig. 7-25)**

Photo Courtesy of Mike Tucker.

Fig. 7-25
On this reproduction bonnet made by Mike Tucker, rectangular pieces of ermine hide have been glued over the ends of the horsehair tassels. The fur pieces were carefully cut so that the hair lies lengthwise when placed on the feather tips.

However, before applying the spots, you may wish to add small fluffies. Actually, some bonnets (particular modern ones) have only a colored fluffy on each tip instead of or in addition to a horsehair bunch. An interesting substitute for fluffies and/or horsehair is the use of one or more dyed rooster hackles per tip.

Quilled Strips
A striking addition to any warbonnet feather is a thin rawhide strip that has been decorated with dyed porcupine quills. The strip is quilled, then it is secured at the bottom, center, and top of the strip by tying it with sinew to the main quill of the feather. This was not common ornamentation, but examples survive from Northern Plains tribes. **(Fig. 7-26a & Fig. 7-26b)**

Buffalo Bill Historical Center, Cody, Wyoming, U.S.A.; Gift of Mrs. Arline Keefe, NA.205.67

Fig. 7-26a
Sioux war bonnet, ca. 1890. This bonnet is made from an assortment of feathers from both immature and mature golden eagles. The front feathers are adorned with porcupine quill wrapped rawhide strips.

Photo by Mike Kostelnik

Fig. 7-26b
Like this Blackfoot style example, many Straight Up bonnets incorporated porcupine quill wrapped rawhide strips attached to the quills of the main feathers.

Other Feather Decorations

Again we should point out how many bonnets exhibit unique decorative attributes. The most obvious pertains to how some bonnets had a mix of immature golden eagle feathers (the white feathers with black tips) and mature (feathers that are all black). Sometimes only the center feather was black. Other instances show alternating sections of immature and mature. Rare examples have all immature feathers, but they are dyed red. It should be noted that, if a bonnet maker did not have enough tail feathers, he might substitute wing feathers. This resulted in the tail feathers being used in the forward half of the bonnet and wing feathers being used in the sides and back.

Many Nez Perce bonnets and those of neighboring tribes have a spot or rectangular piece of ermine fur or fluffy placed in the middle of the quill, half way between the base and tip plumes. **(Fig. 7-27a & Fig. 27b)**

Buffalo Bill Historical Center, Cody, Wyoming, U.S.A.; Chandler-Pohrt Collection, Gift of Mr. and Mrs. Richard A. Pohrt, Sr., NA.203.347

Fig. 7-27b

Gros Ventre bonnet, back. A combination of immature and mature golden eagle tail feathers were used in this bonnet, some of which have been dyed red. Owl (?) feathers, stripped from their quills and dyed red, adorn the top of the crown.

Crown Decorations - Covering the Entire Crown

The warbonnet crown itself can remain completely undecorated. Again, there are historical examples of bonnets where the leather or wool-felt skullcaps have no additional decorations beyond brow bands and side drops. However, decorating the crown can add as much to the overall appearance of your warbonnet as anything else you do.

If you use a wool-felt crown (such as from a hat), then you may have found one that has a pleasing color for you, such as red or yellow. However, any crown can be partly or wholly covered with material which has an interesting color or even fabric design. **(Fig. 7-28)** To completely cover the crown, use the original cloth pattern you made and make a slightly larger version. This should be at least ½" longer than the skull cap along the bottom so that you can fold the edges under for the next step. Sew the covering to the main cap by whip stitching both pieces together along the crown edge.

Buffalo Bill Historical Center, Cody, Wyoming, U.S.A.; Chandler-Pohrt Collection, Gift of Mr. and Mrs. Richard A. Pohrt, Sr., NA.203.347

Fig. 7-27a

Gros Ventre, Ft. Belknap Reservation, Montana, ca. 1890. Rectangular ermine fur pieces have been applied to both the tips and mid-quill on these bonnet feathers.

Partial Crown Decorations

Most bonnets, however, are not completely covered. Usually, fluffy or feather decorations are added to the back of the crown. Still, many bonnets have some kind of material sewn across the front of the bonnet, above the brow band, so that the material shows between the bases of the front feathers. **(Fig. 7-29)** You will note on some old bonnets that this "material" actually is strips of ermine (modern: rabbit) fur. Note: If you chose to glue fabric to the crown, use craft glue and use it sparingly, as too much glue will show up as a hard, dried spot on the fabric.

For convenience, the partial or complete covering must be performed before applying the beadwork, feathers, and side drops.

Buffalo Bill Historical Center, Cody, Wyoming, U.S.A.; NA.205.98

Fig. 7-28
Above: Northern Plains war bonnet, inverted to show the felt crown skull cap completely covered with cotton calico material in a flowered print. The feather wraps are unusual in that the maker used blue velveteen.

Fig. 7-29
Below: Detail of the front of a Southern Cheyenne war bonnet. Ermine fur "fringes" and downy plumes used to cover the front of the crown are readily visible between the feathers. Other decorative touches are the red paint applied to the border of the leather brow band, in addition to edge beading.

Author's Photo. Courtesy of Oklahoma History Museum.

Back Of Crown Decorations

There are a number of attractive ways to decorate the top and back of a bonnet. A common method of covering the bare crown is to sew on a number of small feathers. **(Fig. 7-30)** These can be 4" – 6" plumes, secondary wing feathers, or stripped feathers. These feathers are normally sewn directly to the crown without adding leather loops or firecrackers.

Photo by Joe Rosenthal

Fig. 7-30
Hand-painted imitation red tail hawk feathers were applied to the top of the crown of this reproduction bonnet. These feathers, in addition to the large plumes used on the base of the main bonnet feathers and Major Plume, help give this crown a more finished, interesting look.

Ermine "Fringed Fur" Crown Decorations

With the importance that some Northern tribes attached to the ermine, it is not surprising that bonnet makers found many creative ways to incorporate ermine fur as a crown covering. For this purpose, the ermine fur is prepared by cutting wide sections from an ermine hide and then cutting the pieces along one edge to create "fur fringes". See Chapter XI on Straight Up Bonnets for more information on how to prepare these materials. After the fringed pieces are prepared, they can be stitched to the crown in overlapping layers. **(Fig. 7-31)** A modern day alternative is to use strips of white rabbit fur.

Photo by Mark Miller

Fig. 7-31
Several layers of ermine fur "fringes" were sewn in horizontal overlapping rows to completely cover this bonnet crown.

Major Plume for Crown

On the back of many bonnets, attached to the top of the crown, is often seen a large, single feather or stripped quill. **(Fig. 7-32)** Even though it is usually made from a wing spike (because of a spike's extra strength and length), it is referred to by today's craftsman as a "major plume". Old bonnets in museums that do not have a major plume may yet have had one at an earlier date which has now been lost. Why such a feather was used has yet to be found in the literature, so we do not know its meaning or origin. However, a major plume can be seen on bonnets from different tribes.

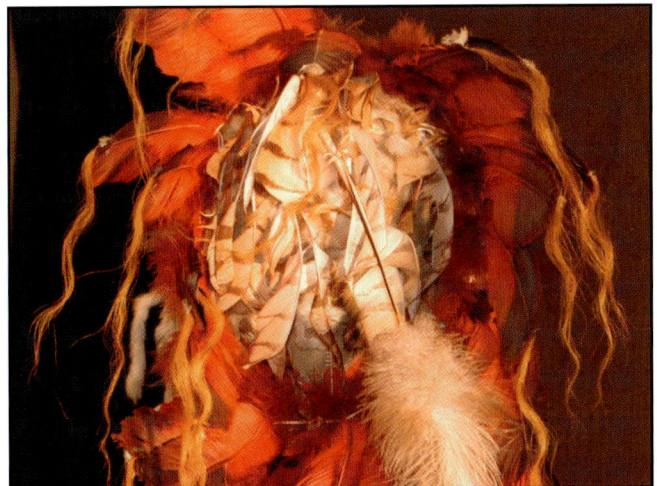

Author's Photo. Courtesy of Oklahoma History Museum.

Fig. 7-32

An old Southern Cheyenne war bonnet, in need of repair, demonstrates the use of red-dyed immature golden eagle feathers to construct the bonnet. Its crown is covered with several owl feathers, the webbing of which has been partly stripped from the upper quill, then that section of the quill cut off. Note the short length of the horsehair tassels.

It is widely assumed that this "plume" is intended to be the personal sign of the owner, to which are attached adornments of special significance to him. For this reason, one is not likely to find feathers decorated the same on more than one bonnet. The decorations might be small fluffs or other feathers, ribbons, beads, hawk bells, fur, etc. However, in modern times, these major plumes have taken on a somewhat universal appearance, usually with large base and tip fluffies.

Pompons

A number of historical photos show a unique center feather at the front of the bonnet that might be described as a fluffie or hackle-covered quill. **(Fig. 7-33 & Fig. 7-34)** Though rarely seen on modern warbonnets, this item is quite striking. It resembles a decorative feathered shaft, called a pompon, worn both today and in centuries past on a style of non-Indian military and band uniform hat called a shako. The author was unable to find specific information describing its construction in the literature, but in the many photos that were examined, it appears they were made from a single large quill (or perhaps a slender stick) that was bound in a spiral fashion with dyed rooster hackles or fluffies. These pompons most often show up on warbonnets worn by Sioux and Blackfoot men, but examples are also seen among Crow and other tribes.

Print from Author's Collection

Fig. 7-33

Kicks Iron, Lakota, wears a war bonnet with a fluffy-decorated pompon visible at the top center of the headdress. Frank Friske photo, ca. 1905.

Print in author's collection.

Fig. 7-34

This painting by Wienhold Reiss (1886-1953) demonstrates the striking effect of a bright red pompon fashioned from dyed rooster hackles. The wearer is No Runner, Blackfoot, whose Straight Up bonnet is constructed of mature golden eagle feathers. Reiss' paintings of many Blackfoot subjects were used on calendars issued by the Great Northern Railway to help lure passengers for trips to the West.

Before Indians were congregated on reservations and subsequently surrounded by agrarian settlers, it might be assumed that they had no access to rooster hackles. However, inventories of trading concerns show that elaborate ostrich, peacock, and other plumes were very popular with the Indians, and it is possible that rooster hackles were included as trade items. We also know from Catlin (1830s) that some Indians who visited Washington, DC had occasion to acquire complete pompons. In addition, surplus military uniforms and parts were given or traded to Indians beginning with early European contact.

Trailers

A man who had an abundance of coup feathers could elect to display them by adding a trailer to his basic warbonnet. **(Fig. 7-35)** These feathers would be decorated like the other bonnet feathers, then strung together in one or two "trailers" down a piece of material attached to the back of the crown. They also are laced together with a secondary lace. Trailers made from both tail and secondary wing feathers are in collections.

Author's Photo. Courtesy of Oklahoma History Museum.

Fig. 7-35

Southern Cheyenne single trailer bonnet. Trailer material is two pieces of saved list red broadcloth sewn together, the undyed edges of which are seen at the end and middle of the trailer. Such long-tailed bonnets were especially showy when the owner road horseback, and they dragged on the ground when he walked.

For a single trailer bonnet, the basic warbonnet is constructed as usual, with the crown feathers spaced and tied together in a complete circle with the secondary lace. A large piece of cloth (often "trade cloth") or tanned leather is sewn to the back bottom of the crown, to which are then laced the trailer feathers. The secondary lace of the trailer feathers is then tied to the crown feather circle at the point where the ends of the crown secondary lace is tied together. (**Fig. 7-36**) The effect is that the trailer feathers stand out when the bonnet is worn.

Author's Photo. Courtesy of Oklahoma History Museum.

Fig. 7-36

Detail of Fig. 7-35 showing how trailer was attached to the crown at several places by using leather tie thongs.

A double trailer bonnet has two different methods of construction. In one, we find that, instead of tying the crown feathers together in a circle, the trailer feathers on each side are tied in such a manner as to be a continuation of the bonnet feathers as they come off the crown. (**Fig. 7-37**) In the second style, the customary feather circle is created on the bonnet, then the two trailers of feathers are tied into the side feathers of the crown. (**Fig. 7-38**)

Buffalo Bill Historical Center, Cody, Wyoming, U.S.A.; Adolf Spohr Collection, Gift of Larry Sheerin, NA.205.3

Fig. 7-37

Back of the Shoshone horned bonnet shown in Fig. 6-1. In this style of double trailer construction, the trailers are a continuation of the crown feathers. The trailer has been split up almost midway to facilitate the bonnet's display during horseback riding.

Historically, trailers were made either from tanned leather (usually not too soft but with some body) or heavy material. The fabric trailer sometimes had a stiff backing of rawhide or at least one or more additional layers of material to give it a flattened shape. Although not especially necessary for the single trailer bonnet, the double trailer style benefited from having a stiff trailer base to allow the two rows of feathers to stay separated. A double trailer variation was to have the actual fabric trailer split half way up or more from the bottom. This allowed the left and right feather trailers to fall on either side of a horse's rump when the rider was mounted. Even when walking, the split trailer will have added movement with each stride of the wearer.

The fabric trailers themselves also could be decorated. For starters, old trailers often were made from red saved list cloth, with the undyed white edge at the bottom. Then, the edges of the fabric often were bound with binding of silk, trade wool, or other fabric. Today, a good binding is Fox Braid, available in several colors. Once the trailer is bound, other fluffs, small secondary raptor feathers, sequins, ermine or rabbit strips, hawk bells, etc. can be attached to the material. **(Fig. 7-39)** Ribbons can be sewn down or attached as streamers, lane stitch beadwork designs can be added, and so on.

Buffalo Bill Historical Center, Cody, Wyoming, U.S.A.; Gift of Pauline Hills and Thelma Crandall, NA.205.74

Fig. 7-38

Northern Plains Double Trailer bonnet, ca. 1905. 21 eagle feathers encircle the felt hat crown. On each side of the trailer, a set of 23 feathers is attached to the secondary lace of the crown feathers. This example also demonstrates the use of split trailer material.

Author's Photo. Courtesy of Oklahoma History Museum.

Fig. 7-39

Detail of the Southern Cheyenne bonnet in Fig. 7-18 showing how the trailer has been sewn to the back of the bonnet crown. A circle of metal sequins decorates the trailer.

Note: Because of the added weight from the trailers, these bonnets often had leather tie thongs on the crown, such that they could be tied under the chin to better keep the bonnet in position.

Trailer Bonnets: Different Styles

There can often be seen differences in Northern and Southern Plains trailer bonnet styles. Following are some photos showing the flared style in Crow and Northern Cheyenne bonnets, and an historic photo of a Southern Plains leader, Quanah Parker, who wears a swept back style. Also see the Southern bonnet in Chapter VIII, worn by both Lone Wolf, Kiowa, and Wild Horse, Comanche.

Fig. 7-40 — Bud Lake & Randy Brewer Crow Collection

Fig. 7-41 — Bud Lake & Randy Brewer Crow Collection

Front and back views of 5 Crow men wearing beautiful flaring trailer bonnets and ready for a parade. Each trailer appears to be two separate pieces instead of one that has been split. Both styles of trailer-to-crown attachment are evident.

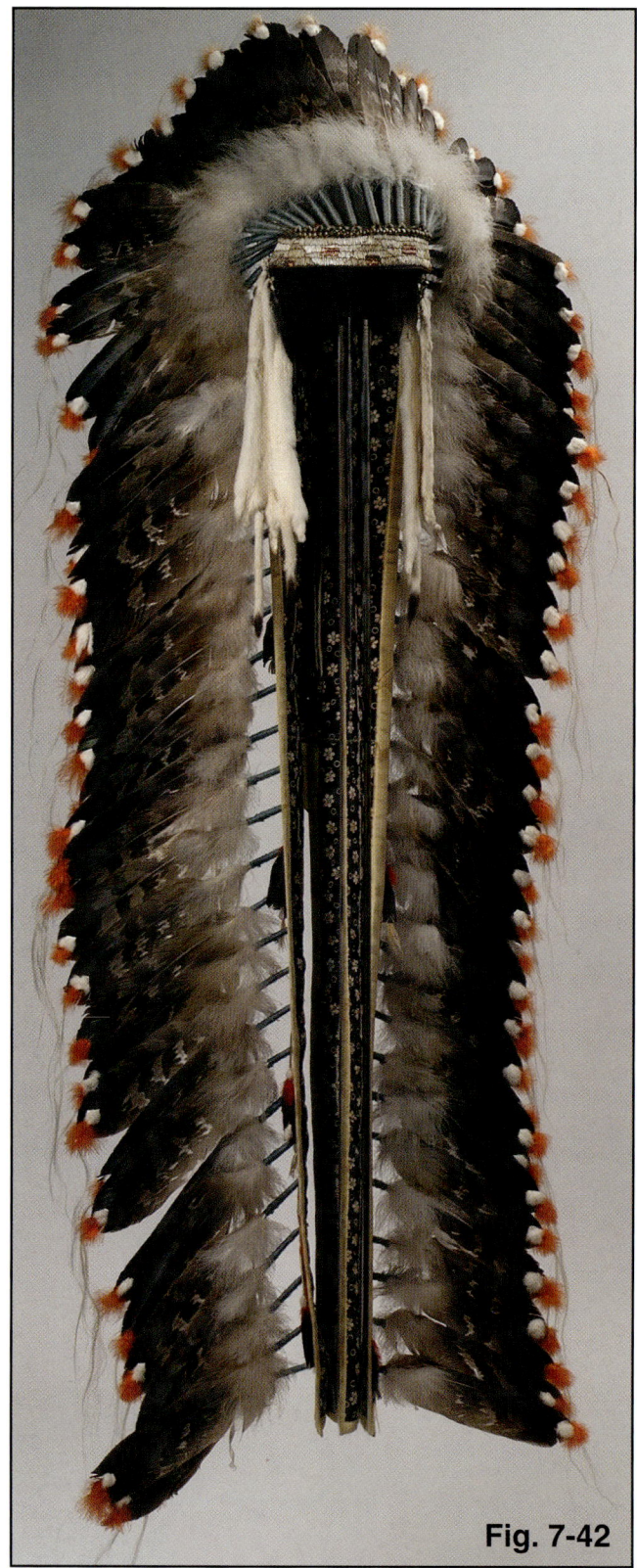

Fig. 7-42

Buffalo Bill Historical Center, Cody, Wyoming, U.S.A.;
Dr. Robert L. Anderson Collection, NA.205.9

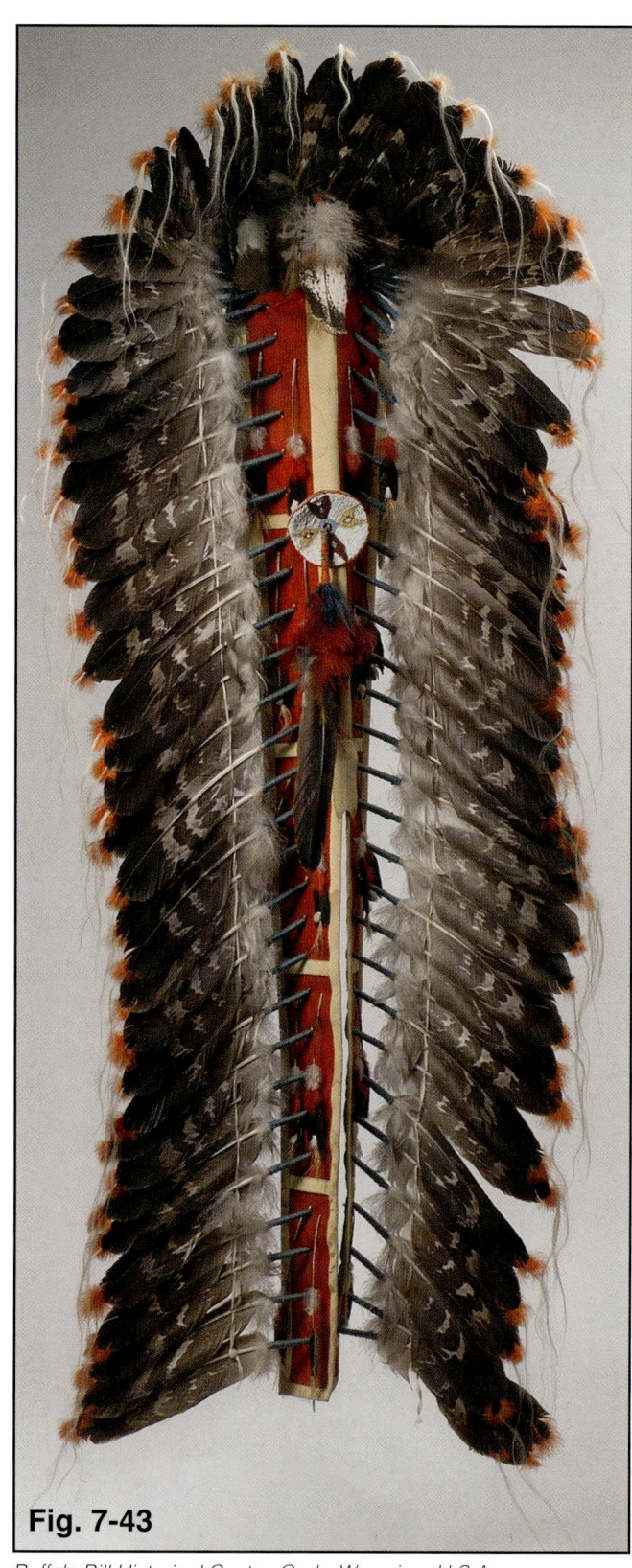

Fig. 7-43

Buffalo Bill Historical Center, Cody, Wyoming, U.S.A.;
Dr. Robert L. Anderson Collection, NA.205.9

Fig. 7-42 & Fig. 7-43: Northern Cheyenne Double Trailer Warbonnet, ca. 1900. Made from mature golden eagle tail feathers mounted on a skull cap of commercial leather. The base of each feather is wrapped with blue yarn, instead of cloth. The split red cloth trailer is backed with a black floral print cloth, then its edges bound with yellow grosgrain ribbon. A large beaded medallion accents the center of the trailer.

Fig. 7-44 Buffalo Bill Historical Center, Cody, Wyoming, U.S.A.; Dr. Robert L. Anderson Collection, NA.205.9

Detail of the porcupine quillwork brow band and bead decorations of the bonnet in the previous Figures.

Fig. 7-45 DeGolyer Library, Central University Libraries, Southern Methodist University, Dallas, Texas. Quanah Parker ag2008.005.8.1.155.r.parker

The renowned Comanche chief, Quanah Parker, rides at a celebration in southern Oklahoma in the early 1900s. His warbonnet is typical of Swept Back Southern Plains headdresses. Quanah carries a fully beaded spear with a large pompon on the end, typical of others used by Comanche men of the period.

Missouri Valley Special Collections, Kansas City Public Library, Kansas City, Missouri.

A Note About Photographs 8

Missouri Valley Special Collections, Kansas City Public Library, Kansas City, Missouri.

It has long been observed by researchers that historic photographs cannot always be taken at face value. Old West photographers were in business to sell photographs to the general public, and they learned early on that "the public" wanted to see Indians not only in their native dress but wearing warbonnets and war paint. So, a number of those photographers acquired warbonnets, tobacco bags, bows and arrows, shields, etc. and used them repeatedly as studio props. Thus, when reviewing several Indian images by the same photographer, it is not uncommon to see the same warbonnet, war shirt, weapon, etc. being worn or held by several different Indian subjects. Further, the same article may be worn by Indians of different tribes, such that we may discover a photo of a Crow Indian wearing a Sioux war shirt, for example. Therefore, the student of Indian material culture must keep this in mind when examining old photos for clues to construction details. Perhaps the best approach is to look at as many different photos as possible and draw tentative conclusions based on what appears to be the norm. This is another example why it is important to immerse one's self as much as possible in the study of Indian material culture if one expects to be able to faithfully recreate items in the Indian style or style of a particular tribe.

Constructing A Basic Warbonnet

Please read all the information before beginning.

Materials

Following are materials to make a Plains Warbonnet with 30 feathers. (Materials for optional items, such as ermine tubes and a pompon, are not included.) The craftsman can substitute for many of the listed materials, based on the previous discussion of warbonnet components. (Note: If you wish to make a Trailer Bonnet – either a Single or Double Trailer – you will need an additional minimum of 15 feathers per Trailer. See Construction information for Trailer Bonnets in Chapter 10.)

30 Imitation Eagle Feathers
1 oz. 5" – 6" base plumes
½ oz. 2"-3" tip plumes
1 **Wing Spike** – For Major Plume (May substitute a 1/8" x 12" wood dowel)
1 piece 2 ½" x 24" red wool or wool felt
2 pieces stiff thin leather or rawhide: 4 ½" x 4 ½" (or 1 piece 4 ½" x 8") – for leather loops
½" oz. 12" – 14" horsehair (optional)
1 **bonnet crown:** May be made from leather pieces sewn together, a commercial wool-felt hat crown, or an old wool-felt hat.
1 1 ¼" x 10" Beaded/Quilled Brow band
2 **Medallions:** 1 ½" or 2" diameter, either Beaded or Quilled (may substitute Quilled Wheels)

1 36" Soft leather/buckskin lace – for Primary Lace
2 **Bobbins** heavy cotton thread (e.g., Button & Carpet thread)
1 **Spool** of colored thread (Recommended: white or yellow) – for "Firecracker" thread wraps
6' – 8' **Simulated Sinew** – For Secondary Lace. Can substitute heavy string, such as "kite string" If Simulated Sinew is used, acquire the full-thickness type.
1 **White Rabbit Fur** – Grade A (few or no holes)
1 **Bottle** of craft glue
1 **Roll** of Masking Tape (optional)
4 1/8" x 36" Wood Dowels

Tools

Scissors (very sharp)
Awl
Xacto® or pen knife
Sewing needle
Darning needle (very large sewing needle)
Pliers
Medium grit (120) sandpaper
Rulers: 12" straight ruler, yard stick, AND one cloth measuring tape
Pencil
Tailor's chalk
Small artist's brush (optional)

Making The Warbonnet

Crown

Leather Crown **(Fig. 9-1)** Making a crown begins by first measuring the circumference of your head with a cloth tape measure.

Photo by Joe Rosenthal

Fig. 9-1

4-Piece leather crown with brow band, major plume, and feather lacing slits. Made and photographed by Joe Rosenthal

How you choose to wear your bonnet (either pulled forward or pulled back) will contribute to how the bonnet feathers fall. Once this decision is made, measure around your head from just above the eyebrows, across the horizontal ridge of bone across the bottom back of your skull just above the neck, and back to the front. The crown should be a little loose and may even cover the tops of your ears, so add enough to your measurement to accommodate this. A good place to start is so that two fingers can fit easily under the circumference measurement. You may also find it helpful in constructing the crown to know the measurement across the head from ear to ear (remembering that you may want the crown to overlap the ears).

For the Swept Back Style, the back section must be longer by 1" than the sides or front. Plan accordingly if you make your own bonnet crown. For example, if you use an old hat, the back of the crown should extend 1" onto the brim in a graceful curve. **(Fig. 9-2a)**

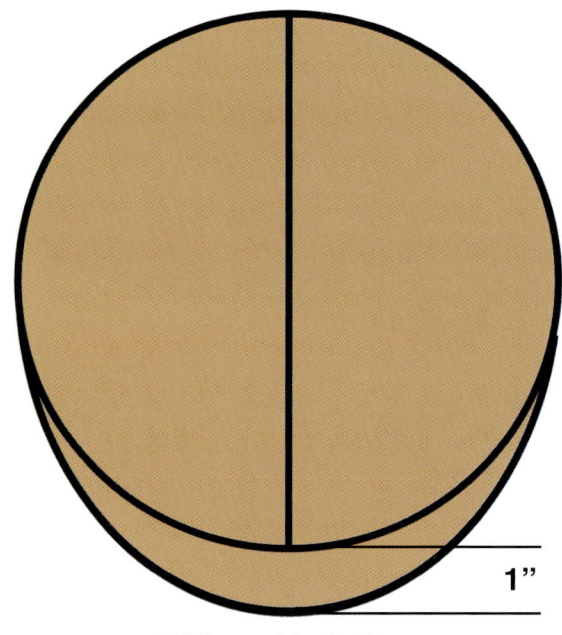

Fig. 9-2a **2 Piece Variation**
Crown

Swept-back style crown showing extension at back.

A two piece crown will have the seam running down the center of the head, from front to back. A three piece crown consists of a rectangular center strip about 3" wide that runs from front to back, on each side of which are sewn two symmetrical half-circles. This is a good crown style for making a bonnet with an elongated back for the Swept Back bonnet. In this case, the two side pieces will not be symmetrical but will have the back ends elongated compared to the front half of each "semi-circle". A four piece crown has 4 pie-shaped pieces sewn together. **(Fig. 9-2b, c, & d)**

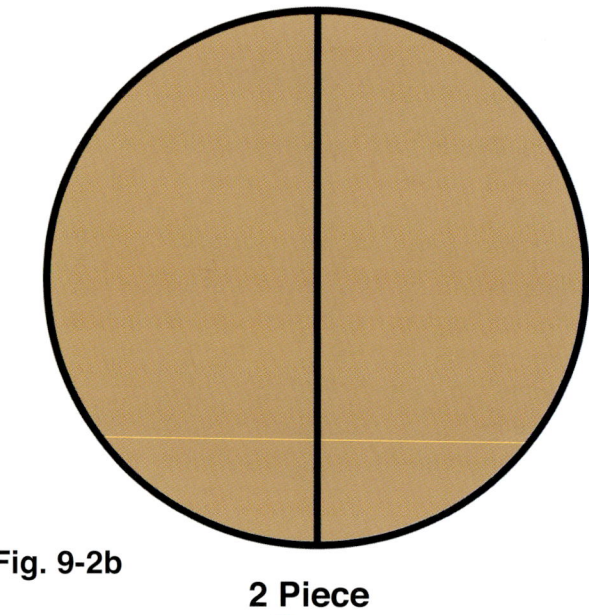

Fig. 9-2b

2 Piece
Crown

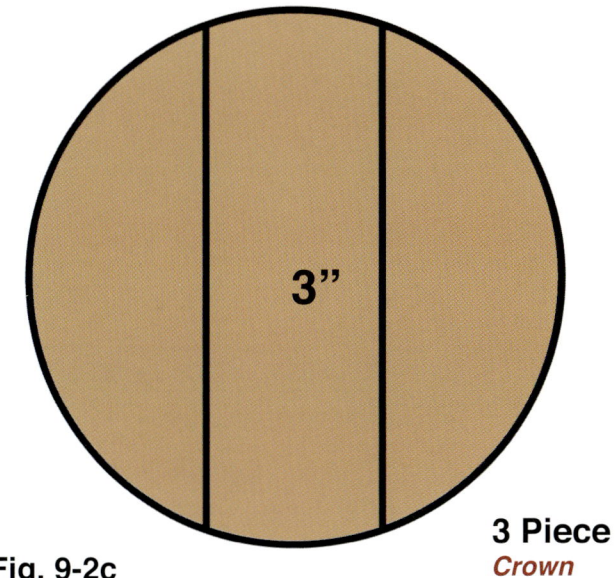

Fig. 9-2c **3 Piece** *Crown*

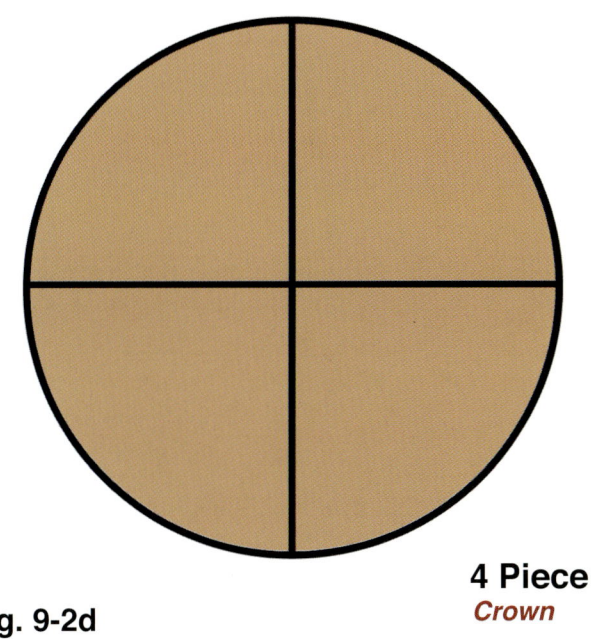

Fig. 9-2d **4 Piece** *Crown*

Once you are satisfied with the fit of your pattern, take it apart and transfer the shapes to leather for the crown by outlining each piece with pencil (not ink). (Note: It is ALWAYS best to pre-stretch leather before you make any kind of garment article from it. Soak the hide in water, then stretch it as tight as possible while tacking it to a board. When dry, soften the leather by rubbing it between your hands.) Warning: Crowns made from unstretched leather are likely to become misshapen over time, resulting in a poor-fitting warbonnet.

Cut out the pieces, then sew them together with a not-too-snug whipstitch. Note: If you pull the stitches tight, you will end up with ridges along the seams. When sewn with just a little bit of slack, the seams can be pressed flat when you are finished.

Felt Crown

If you are using a manufactured felt crown or old felt hat, it probably will need to be trimmed to the proper length and then sized by reducing the circumference to fit your head. For an old hat, remove the inside liner and outside sweat band, then cut off the brim, but, if you are making a Swept Back bonnet, only cut off the front 2/3rds of the brim (from behind the ears on one side, all around to behind the ears on the other). You will need a portion of the back for the crown extension discussed earlier. **(Fig. 9-2a)**

A cloth pattern (see above) can be helpful to cut and re-size pre-fabricated crowns. Place the pattern inside the crown and use chalk to mark the crown where it needs to be cut. If you choose not to use a pattern, first try on the crown (hat) to see how it fits. It will need to be marked and cut in 2 steps to (a) establish the circumference and, (b) reduce the circumference. First, have a friend mark the crown around the circumference where it will need to be trimmed for length (i.e.,

Decide whether you want a two, three, or four piece cap, then take your circumference measurement, divide it by the number of pieces in the crown (if 2 or 4 pieces), and plot out a paper pattern for each of the parts. (For a 3 piece crown with 3" center strip, subtract 6" from the head circumference and divide by 2: this will give you the bottom dimension for each of the two side pieces.) Then use these patterns to cut identical pieces from scrap cloth (anything that has some thickness but is non-stretchy will do, like felt or blanket scraps). Staple the pieces together with flat seams, try on the resulting skull cap, then adjust your pattern accordingly.

how far down on your head it fits). Note that, when the crown is laid flat with the front center on top, you will probably be cutting the crown in a curved line. **(Fig. 9-3)**

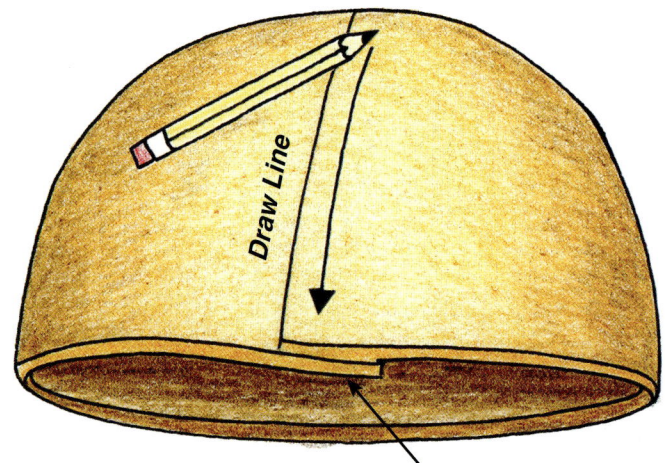

Fig. 9-4b

Use chalk to mark the line where the edges overlap. Cut off the excess.

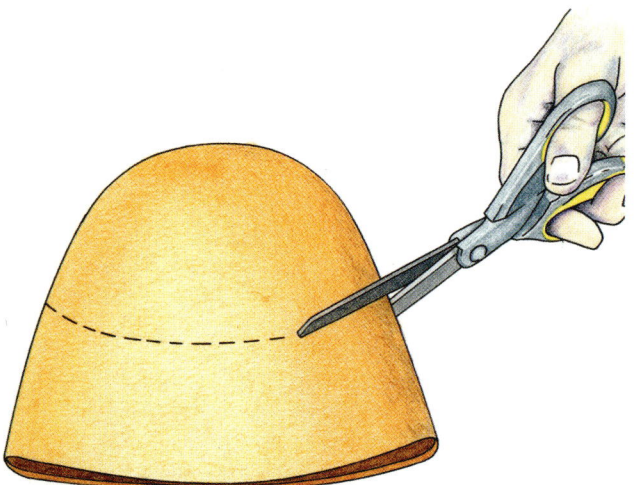

Fig. 9-3

Head was measured from front to back, then from ear to ear. Dimensions transferred to crown and line drawn connecting marks.

This will result in a crown that appears even all around when worn. Cut along this line. Now, put the crown back on and, if it is too large in circumference, trim and sew as per **Fig. 9-4a through c.** Remember that the crown should be a little loose, and you should be able to place 1-2 fingers under the crown edge.

Fig. 9-4c

Whipstitch edges together to make a flat seam. Seam will go down back of head.

The crown for a Swept Back Bonnet needs to retain a 1" extension of material onto the back brim like a very small duck bill, so include this consideration in your measurements and cutting.

Brow Band

After making the crown, decide whether you want the bottom edge of the brow band to be sewn to the bottom of the crown or if it is to extend below the edge of the crown. **(See Fig. 9-1)**

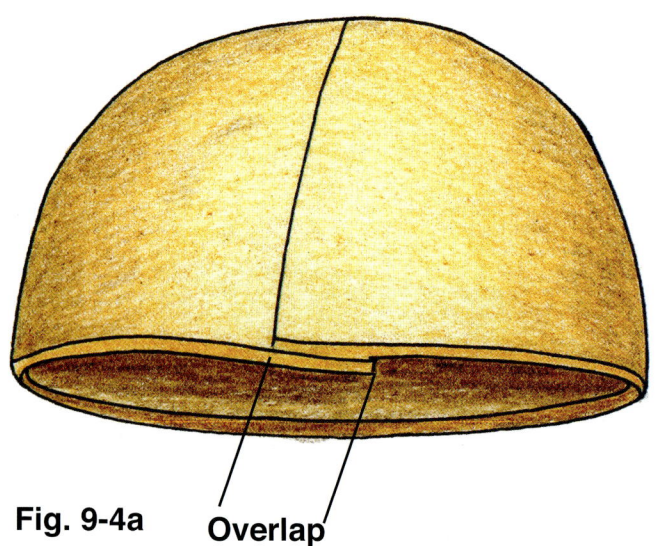

Fig. 9-4a **Overlap**

For crown with circumference that is too large, start by making a cut from one edge to the top center. Try on crown and overlap cut edges to find proper circumference.

A beaded band positioned above the crown edge **(Fig. 9-5)** should be sewn with stitches made between the 2nd and 3rd rows of beads along all sides of the strip. For a beaded band that extends below the edge of the crown, the beadwork should first be sewn to a thin piece of leather. (Use the same technique as above to sew inside the rows.) This is how the historic pieces were made. The leather helps the beadwork maintain its shape and absorbs much of the sweat, all of which otherwise would get on the bead threads and cause them to rot. After sewing the beadwork to the leather, attach the brow band to the crown with a running stitch around both sides and top border of the leather, going through both the leather and crown with each stitch. Many old pieces actually show that 3-5 beads were added to each stitch to give added decoration to the brow band. Edge-beading of this leather piece before it is sewn on was also a common practice. **(Fig. 9-6 & Fig. 7-14)**

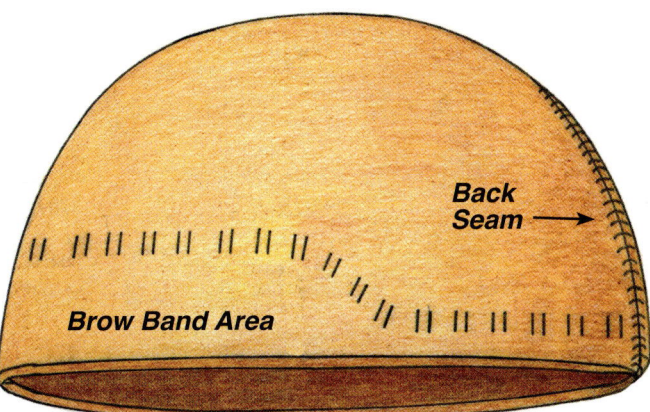

Fig. 9-5

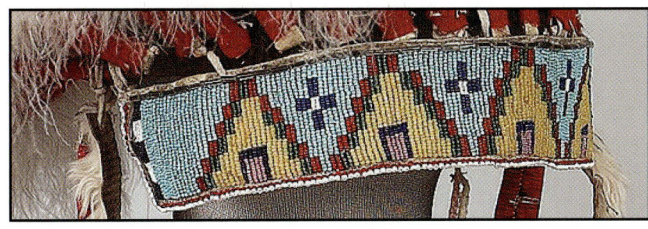

BBHC   NA 203.934

Fig. 9-6

Drops and/or Beaded Rosettes

We recommend that you wait until the bonnet feathers are attached before sewing on any drops and medallions. Otherwise, the drops will get in the way. However, at this time, it is good to position the medallions where they will be (usually with approximately half of the medallion covering the end of the brow band), then use a pencil to draw a light line on the crown around the outside edge of the medallion. This will give you a reference line around which to place the feather slits. When finished, set the crown aside until the feathers are prepared.

FEATHER PREPARATION
Feather Anatomy

In the following instructions, we will use terms for the various parts of a feather. **(Fig. 9-7)** The **Quill** is the main shaft of the feather, while **Web** or Webbing refers to the thin, soft material on either side of the quill. The end of the feather where the quill is the thinnest is referred to as the **Tip** or **Top**, and the thickest end of the quill is referred to as the **Base** or **End** of the feather. In determining which side of the feather is the **Front** or **Back**, note that the webbing on one side has a slight gloss, while the other side has a "flat", dull surface finish. We refer to the glossy side as the **Front** and the dull side as the **Back**. This is especially evident in natural feathers like those on old warbonnets.

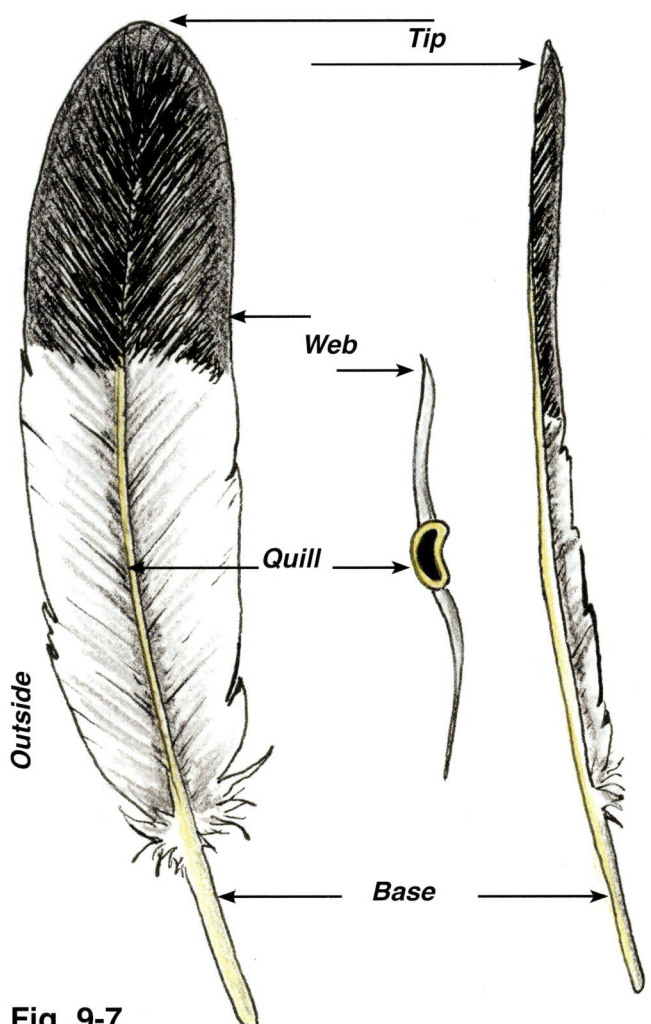

Fig. 9-7

Another feature of the feather has to do with which of the bird's wings – left or right – the feather comes from. Every turkey wing feather has a slight curve to the quill. When looking at it from the front, if it curves to the left, it comes from the left wing, and vice versa for right curved feathers. You will also notice that, often, there is more webbing on the inside of the curve. Below, the terms **Lefts** and **Rights** refer to the feathers that come from the respective left or right wing. In **Fig. 9-7**, judging from the curve of this feather and looking at it from the Front, this is a **Right** wing feather.

Center Feather

The tail feathers of raptors, such as eagles, contain an even number of feathers. **(See Fig. 7-1 and Fig. 7-3)** However, the two feathers in the middle are straight. These are commonly referred to as Center Feathers. These feathers have a straight quill and a near-equal amount of webbing on both sides of the quill. **(Fig. 9-8)** In other words, they appear symmetrical. Wings, however, do not have a center feather, and this includes turkey wing feathers from which the Imitation Eagle feathers are made. So, if you want your bonnet to have a single Center Feather (and, therefore, an odd number of total feathers), then you should select an appropriate turkey wing feather and trim it so that its webbing is symmetrical. You first will have to straighten the quill before trimming the web. (See below for information on Trimming Feathers.)

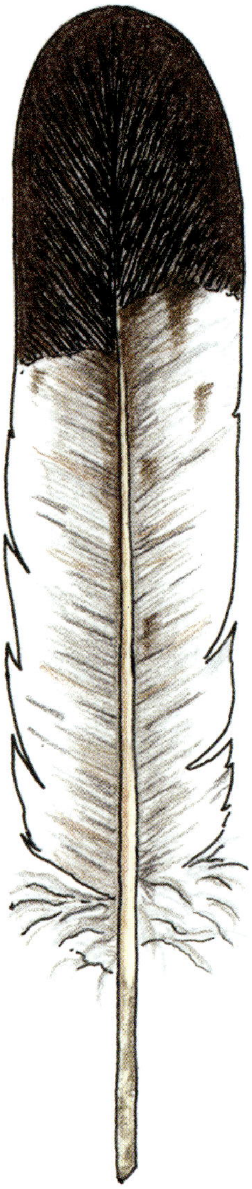

Fig. 9-8

Nearly bilaterally symmetrical center tail feather.

Feather Sorting

Determine which feathers are Lefts and which are Rights, and divide them into the two groups. There should be an equal number for each side (15 in this example), plus a center feather, if desired. **(Fig. 9-9)**

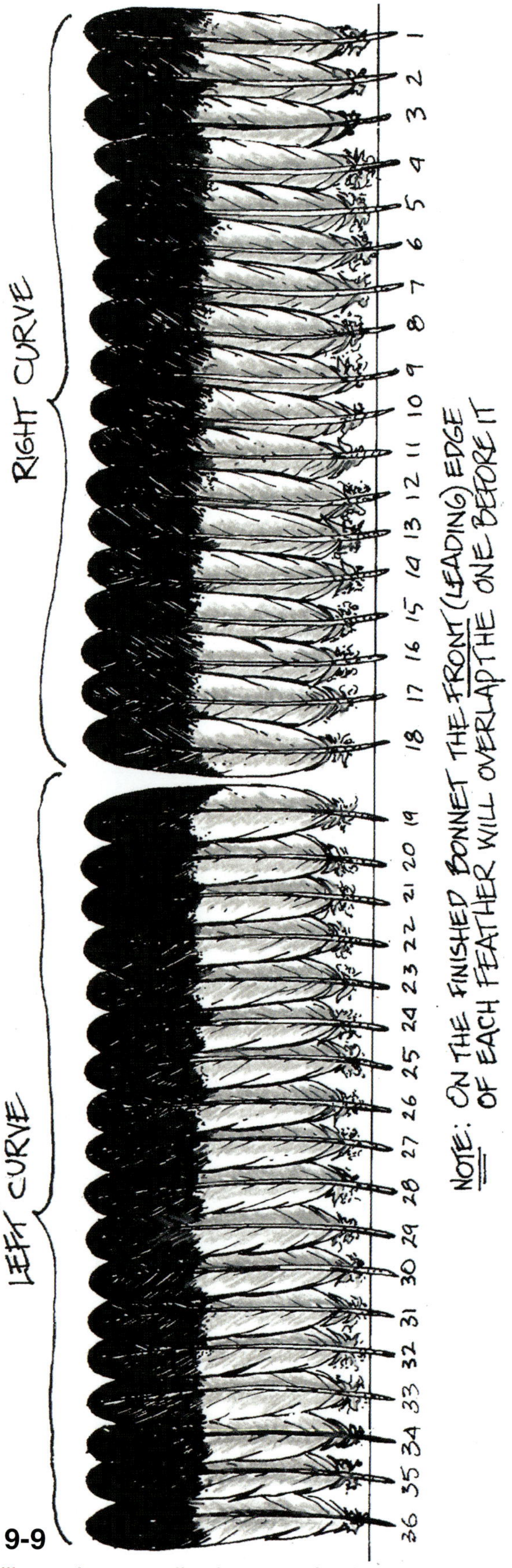

Fig. 9-9

This illustration actually shows 36 feathers (18 lefts and 18 rights) with no center feathers.

Note on Trailer Feathers: All the feathers in a trailer should be from the same side, with a Double Trailer having one trailer of Lefts and one of Rights. Usually the shortest feathers from an entire batch are used for the trailers, so keep this in mind when you originally purchase and sort your feathers. Each trailer consists of a minimum of 15 feathers spaced 2" apart. However, you may want more feathers in your trailer for greater effect or because you are tall.

Straightening

The quills of most real eagle feathers have less curve or a different curvature than turkey feathers. Therefore, you will need to straighten your turkey feathers to get the best results. There are two basic methods for straightening the quills: heating and crimping. Heating is a tedious process and, if you are not carful, you can over-heat the webbing, causing it to curl. However, heating will not mar the quill like crimping does. We will describe both methods.

Heating

Option 1: Hold the feather at both ends and run the quill over a bare light bulb (no more than 100 watts) as shown in **Fig. 9-10.** You may wish to protect your eyes with sunglasses because of the total time it takes to straighten all the feathers. Heating the quill on both front and back will give the best results. As the quill begins to soften, gently apply steady pressure to it as you move it back and forth over the hot bulb. Attempt to bend the quill so that it is straight both from side to side and from front to back. Once it has achieved the desired shape, hold the quill in that position, away from the bulb, until it has cooled. Note: As you heat the quill, be VERY careful not to touch the webbing to the bulb, or else the webbing may curl.

Option 2: Instead of a bulb, you can use a steam kettle to heat the quill; this also is faster. You should use a kettle with a spout, not an open pan of water. However, the steam will be very hot and can easily curl the webbing if not consistently directed only at the quill. If you wish to use this method, practice first on some waste feathers. As the quill is heated, it must be bent beyond the point where you want it to end up by passing it through the steam until you feel the tension release. When this happens, the quill is softening and can be reshaped. At that time, pull the feather away from the steam and hold it in the desired final position until it cools. Of course, be very careful to not burn yourself on the live steam.

Option 3: Ironing – Turn on the iron with the heat level at the "cotton" or "high" setting. When it is hot, use the iron on a practice feather. It should not mar the quill (causing blisters or burns). If it does, reduce the heat and try again.

When ready, take a feather and hold it by the base as shown with the "top"/glossy side up. Apply the tip of the iron to the quill and gently press the feather down on your ironing surface until the entire web portion is flat. **(Fig. 9-11a & 9-11b)** Heat the quill slowly and carefully. **Note:** Touching the webbing with the iron may damage it.

Fig. 9-10

Fig. 9-11a & 9-11b

Apply only the tip of the iron to the feather quill.

After the quill is sufficiently heated, take both hands and hold the feather so it is straight both up and down and left to right. This will cause the quill to bend in the opposite directions from its natural curve. When satisfied with how the feather is straightened, hold the feather in that position until the quill cools.

Crimping

A faster method for straightening is crimping. To crimp the quill, use thumbnail pressure and make small crimps every 1" or so along the shaft. Start at the bottom and, while pulling the feather at the tip in the desired direction with one hand, crimp with the other. Remember, you need to straighten the quill from left or right and from front to back. Be careful near the tip, as too much pressure will actually break the thin quill. Again, practice first on waste feathers. This method, while fast, will also leave visible crimps. However, most of them will be covered by the fluffs and the other crimps will not noticeable from a short distance away.

Regardless of which method you use, after straightening the feathers, they should lay evenly and flat on the work surface. If any feather does not, re-shape it.

Feather Trimming

This is one of the most important steps in creating an authentic looking bonnet. Turkey feathers do not have the same shapes as eagle feathers, and so they must be trimmed. Most or all of the trimming will be done on the black end.

Probably all of your feathers have ragged-looking tips, so the tip must be trimmed to present a neat end. Also, the quill is exceedingly thin near the tip, and it will be too weak to support the weight of horsehair. If you plan to use horsehair, then trim the quill down to where the quill starts to be stiff. This may be as much as 1" from the natural tip.

Lay out the straightened feathers, Lefts and Rights. Then arrange the feathers from the longest to the shortest for each side. Take the shortest feather from one side, then clip off the tip with a very sharp pair of scissors **(Fig. 9-12)** If you will not use horsehair, cut the tip just below the ragged part of the tip webbing. If horsehair is to be used, cut the tip further down. Note how many inches of black remain on this feather. If you want the finished bonnet to have matched feathers, then trim all the other feathers so that they have the same amount of black (ideally, 3").

Otherwise, clip the tip of each feather below the ragged section (or where the quill is thick enough to support the horsehair tassels).

Fig. 9-12

First step in trimming: clip off tip straight across.

Next, trim the webbing of these feathers to resemble the eagle tail feather shapes shown in **(Fig. 9-13)**, always cutting from the tip toward the base of the feather.

Fig. 9-13

Typical feather shapes in an eagle's tail. Feather on far right resembles outside "blade" feathers. Use 2-6 of this shape in back center of bonnet (½ lefts, ½ rights)

If you do not have the skill to cut these different shapes, then practice on waste feathers until you have one with a satisfactory tip. The desired shape is more like the rounded end of a table knife than the extreme point of the natural turkey feather. Then make a template by placing the feather flat on a piece of thin cardboard, and trace the outline with a marker. Cut out that template and use it as a guide to cut all the bonnet feathers. **(Fig. 9-14)** The template may not fit all feathers exactly, but it will be helpful in achieving the desired shape.

COMPLETING FEATHER PREPARATION

Fig. 9-15

Photo by Joe Rosenthal

Steps To Finish The Feathers: From left to right, these are the steps to prepare each feather before it is attached to the bonnet crown.

Extending The Feathers

Real eagle feathers typically were both wider and longer than turkey wing feathers. So, for a nice, uniform look to the bonnet, it is a "must" to extend the feathers to about 14" total length. This requires measuring 12" down from the tip to the quill end, cutting off the excess quill, then gluing a wooden down into the quill end and trimming the dowel so that the total length is 14". **(Fig. 9-16)**

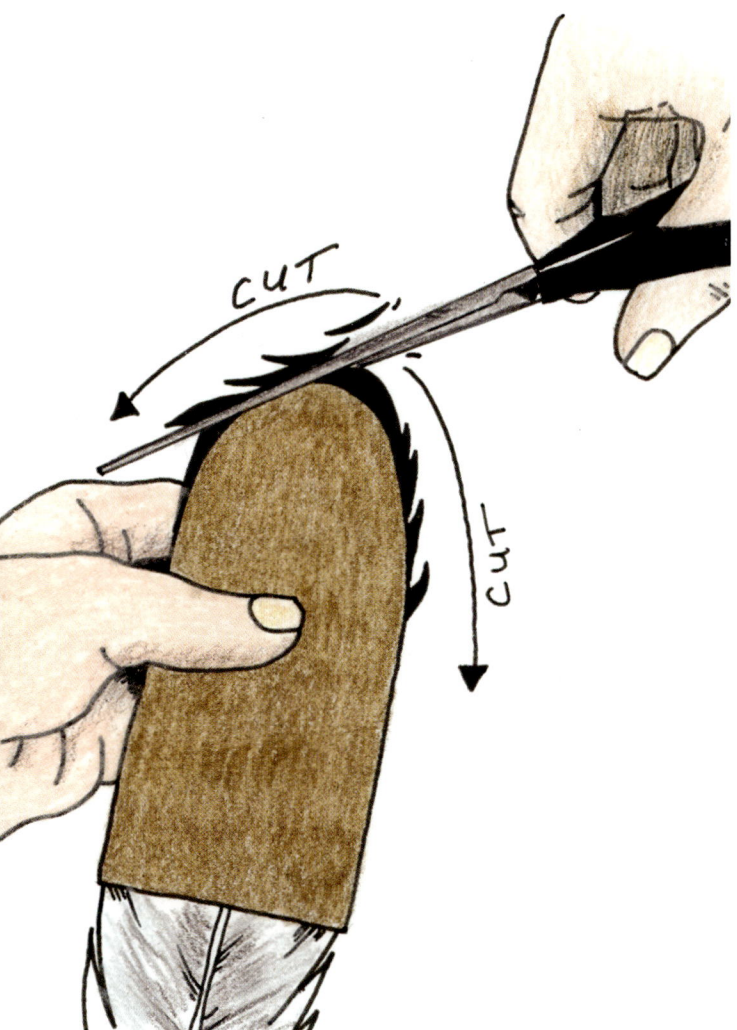

Fig. 9-14

Feather cutting requires very sharp scissors. Cut slowly from the tip toward the base of the feather.

If you are going to have a center feather, pick a turkey feather that has approximately the same amount of webbing on each side of the quill. Then trim it so that the feather is symmetrical.

Fig. 9-16

Tapered wood dowel is inserted into clipped end of quill after applying glue.

After the feather is measured and trimmed, proceed as follows:

1. Start with a full-length dowel (usually 36") and shape a taper on one end with sandpaper and/or a sharp knife. **(Fig. 9-17)**

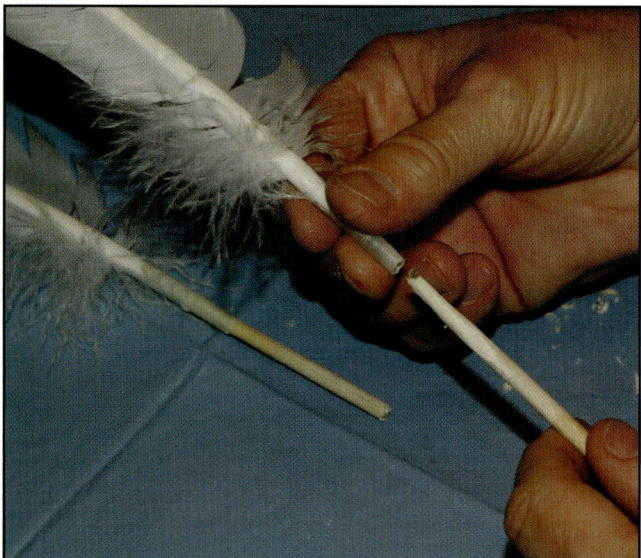

Fig. 9-17 *Photo by Ginger and Rex Reddick*

2. Slip the dowel into the quill as far as it will go without splitting the quill. (If it does split a little, don't worry. The glue will hold it all together) If it does not go in at least ¾", remove the dowel and taper it more.
3. When the tapered end fits satisfactorily, measure from the feather tip down 14" onto the dowel and mark it. Remove the dowel and cut it off.
4. Place glue evenly on the tapered dowel end (use a small artist's brush to spread the glue), then insert the dowel and set the feather aside to dry 2-3 hours. **(Fig. 9-18)**
5. Repeat on all the other feathers.

Fig. 9-18

Wood dowel inserted and glued into quill. Dowel then cut to final length.

Photo by Joe Rosenthal

Option To Equal Lengths

Note: An alternate method to making all the feathers the same length is to graduate them - again, with the use of extensions. Eagle feathers were not all the same size in the bird's tail, with the shortest feathers being on the outside of the tail (sometimes referred to as "blades" because of their resemblance to a table knife). The shorter feathers were reserved for the back of the bonnet (or a trailer).

Before adding dowel extensions, lay the feathers out, Lefts and Rights, and, within each group, placed from the longest to the shortest. The longest feathers (which will be in the front part of the bonnet) should be 14" after being extended, and the shortest feathers in back should be at least 12". So, if you are using 30 feathers, each feather as you go from front to back will be 1/16" shorter then the feather next to it. (2" = 32/16; 32/16 divided by 30 = approximately 1/16") Another way to figure would be to take the total number of feathers on one side (for example, 15) and, if they are to graduate a total of 2" (from 14" to 12"), then size them in small groups of 3: 3 feathers = 14", 3 = 13 ½", 3 = 13", 3 = 12 ½", and 3= 12". You probably will not notice the difference in lengths when the feathers are actually on the bonnet as they graduate from front to back.

Note on Trailer Bonnets —Although the Trailer feathers may be extended to the full 14" length, 12" feathers will usually be satisfactory.

Secondary Lace Holes

You will find it advantageous to now mark and pierce each feather through the back of the quill for the Secondary Lace which will be used later. While the Primary Lace attaches the feather loops to the crown, the Secondary Lace (sometimes referred to as the bridle) actually keeps all the feathers together in uniform position so as to form the "bonnet" effect.

1. Turn the feather over with its back up.
2. From the end of the wood dowel, measure up 4" on the back of the quill and mark it with a pencil.
3. Take an awl and pierce the quill going from side to side through the back. **(Fig.9-19)** The resulting hole (really a "split") should open big enough to later pass the Secondary Lace. If using a buckskin lace, you will benefit from widening the split vertically with a pen knife or Xacto® knife.
4. Mark and pierce all of the bonnet feathers at the 4" distance.

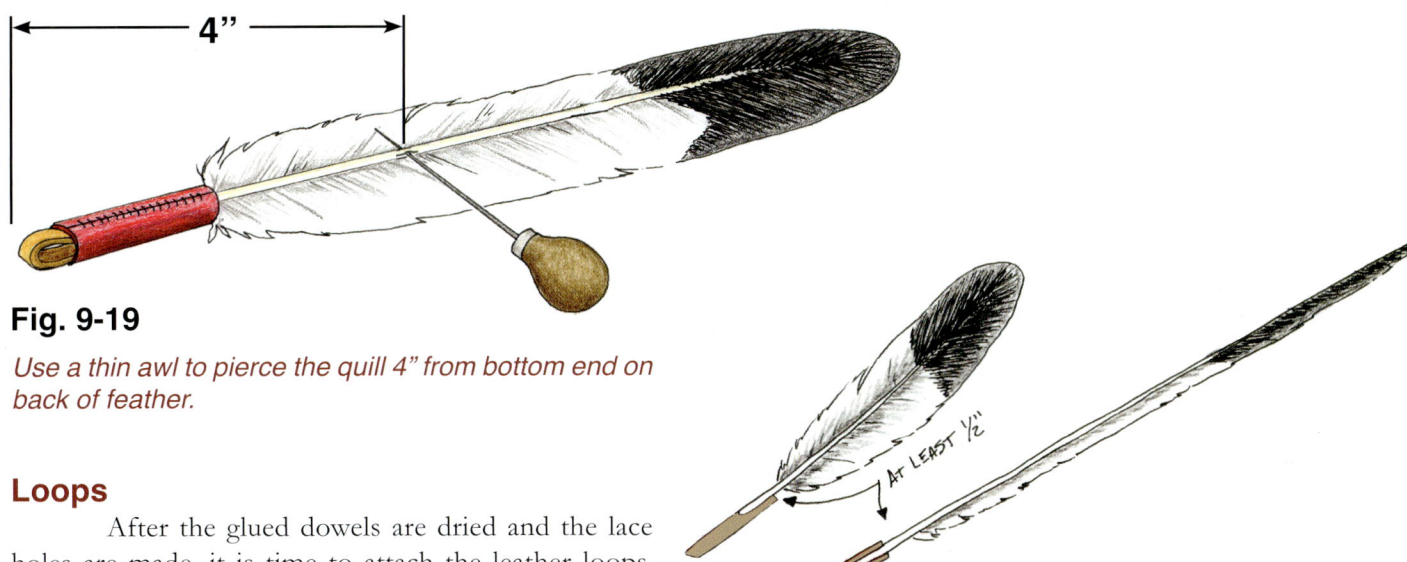

Fig. 9-19

Use a thin awl to pierce the quill 4" from bottom end on back of feather.

Loops

After the glued dowels are dried and the lace holes are made, it is time to attach the leather loops. Stiff leather – even thin rawhide – is much preferred to soft leather. Stiff leather helps the feathers in the front of the bonnet stand up, as you will discover when you lace feathers to the crown.

1. Cut leather strips ¼" x 4 ¼", one for each feather, plus one more for the Major Plume. **(Fig. 9-20)**

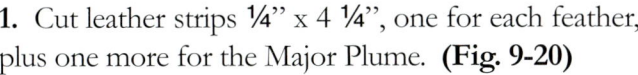

Fig. 9-21

Loop positioning is critical. Note how this loop appears as the feather lays flat.

3. Use a 12"-18" piece of heavy thread, such as Button & Carpet thread, to tightly wrap the leather onto the rawhide. Make sure that the hole in the loop stays parallel with the feather webbing. EXTRA CARE should be taken with this last step: If the loop is not positioned correctly, the feathers will not lay flat against the crown.
4. Prepare all the feathers with leather loops

Rawhide note: If you use actual rawhide, it should be thin enough to be flexible. Dampen the rawhide in order to make it flexible enough to conform to the shape of the quill as it is tied into place. Glue also should be applied to rawhide strips, as described above for tanned leather loops.

Plume (Fluffie or Fluff) Preparation

Next, Base Plumes (Fluffies) will be applied to the feather. Fluffies can be placed on the front only of the feather, but it looks better to have both front and back fluffs.

1. Select 3-5 plumes 5" – 6" long for each feather (depending on whether you want 2 or 3 for the front and 1-2 on the back). A very full effect can be achieved with 3 front plumes and 2 on the back.
2. Most plumes have a second "mini fluff" on the back, growing from the bottom of the quill. Prepare each plume by pulling off the mini fluff, as well as 1" – 2" of the webbing from the base of the large plume itself. **(Fig. 9-22)**

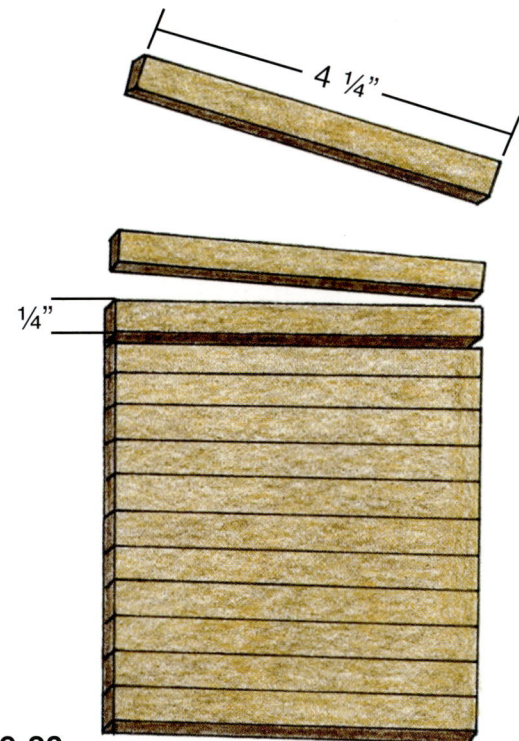

Fig. 9-20

2. Fold a strip in the middle, apply glue to the inside, then position the leather on the end of the dowel. Leave a small space between the dowel end and leather creating a hole just large enough for your lace to pass through (no larger than a pencil). **(Fig. 9-21)**

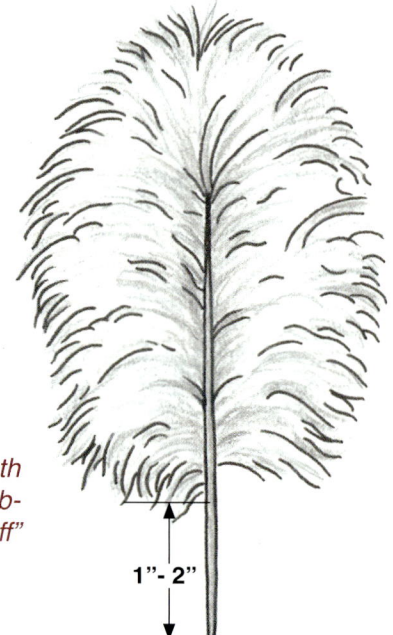

Fig. 9-22

5"-6" plume with both 1"-2" of lower webbing and "mini fluff" removed.

(**Note:** 5"-6" plumes will cover a lot of the "eagle" feather and may be more than you want. If you do not want long base plumes, first cut off the lower quill to make the plume 3 ½", then strip off the lower 1" of the quill.)

3. Apply the appropriate number of fluffs to the front and back. Base plumes can be glued on, tied, taped, or any combination of the three. However, taping is not recommended, as the adhesive will fail over time. If gluing, we recommend doing the fronts of all the feathers, letting them dry, then doing the backs. Position the end of the quill just above the end of the dowel, 1/8" – ¼". To tie, make a couple of thread wraps around the lower part of the loop (just above the loop hole), then continue to thread wrap upward as you add fluffies one at a time. Finish with the thread by tying a couple of clove hitches. **(Fig. 9-23)**

NOTE: Whichever method you use, the distance from the end of the dowel to the top of the wraps MUST be a little less than 2 ½", or else the "firecracker" material will not cover it.

Base Wraps

(Regardless of the methods chosen, we suggest you read all instructions below before beginning.)

1. Cut pieces of red wool or felt into 2 ½" x 1 ½" pieces, enough for all the feathers (including the Major Plume).

2. Wrap a piece of the material around the base of each feather so that it overlaps itself in the back and does not cover the hole in the leather loop. Remember that the 2 ½" dimension goes up and down and the 1 ½" dimension is the wrap-around dimension. **(Fig. 9-24)**

Photo by Joe Rosenthal

Fig. 9-23

Photo by Joe Rosenthal

Fig. 9-24

Front of a feather with material wrapped so that edge is in back.

3. Not all historic or contemporary warbonnets have thread wraps. **(See Fig. 9-24)** However, this feature adds additional visual interest to the finished product.

For thread wraps, first wrap the material as in **Step 2**, then hold the cloth in position with one hand, and now wrap and tie bands of thread near the top and bottom. **(Fig. 9-25)** You should leave an inch or two of the thread sticking out, to be used as a tie when you are through. **(Fig. 9-26)** These bands should be about ¼" wide. **(Fig. 9-27)** Tie off the ends of the thread, then clip off the excess. **(Fig. 9-28)** A drop of glue on the resulting knot will secure the knot for years to come.

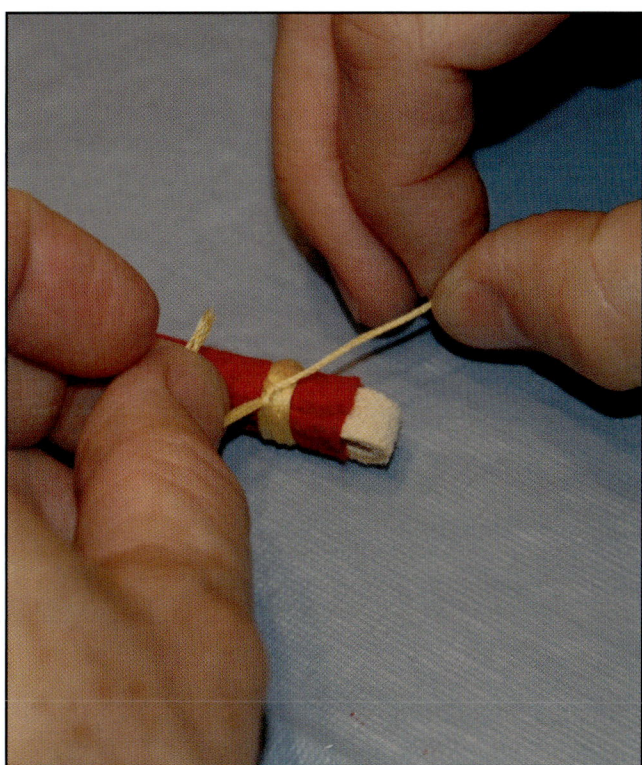

Fig. 9-26 *Photo by Ginger and Rex Reddick*

Finished thread wrap is tied off with knot on back of feather.

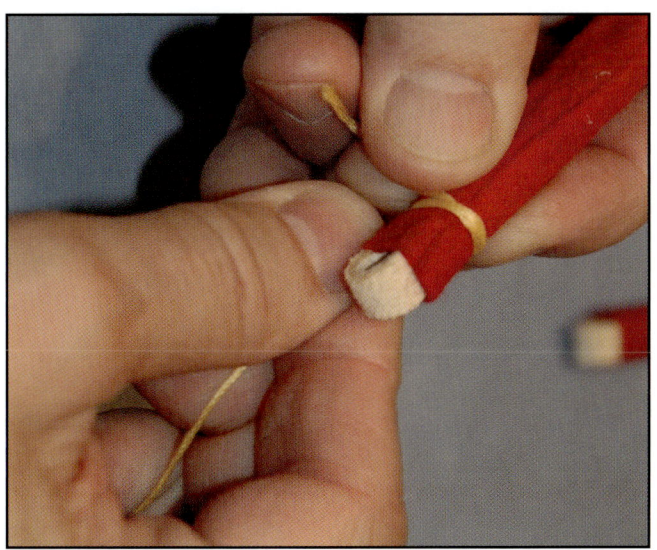

Fig. 9-25 *Photo by Ginger and Rex Reddick*

Start thread wraps approximately ¼" from end of material.

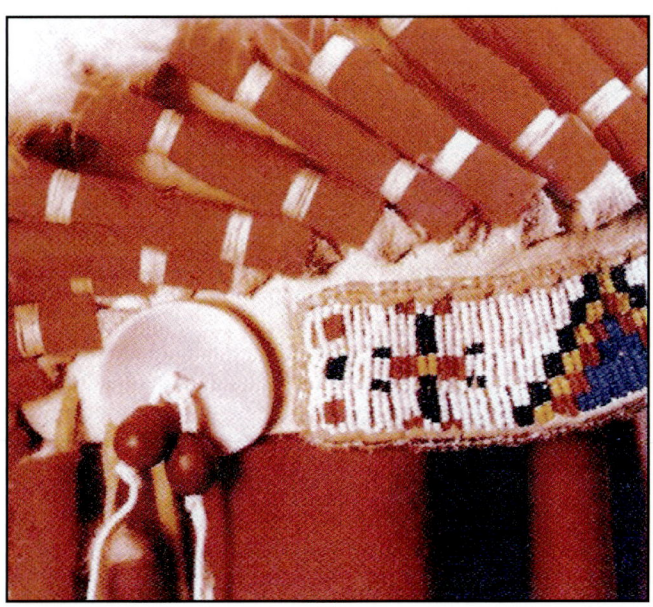

Fig. 9-27 *CCTP Photos*

Finished bonnet with ¼" wide thread wraps.

Fig. 9-28 *Photo by Ginger and Rex Reddick*

Clip thread ends close to knot, then apply drop of glue to knot.

These photos show feathers completed with variations in the use of components such as tip plumes and thread wraps. **(Fig. 9-29 and Fig. 9-30)**

Photo by Joe Rosenthal

Fig. 9-29

Old-style prepared feather with no thread wraps.

Fig. 9-30

Fully-decorated feathers with thread wraps, tip plumes and spots.

Option: Before wrapping the thread bands, you may wish to sew up the back of the red material with red thread. Some "old timers" preferred this technique, and, of course, it is necessary if you decline to use thread wraps. Following is an efficient way to apply "firecrackers" without thread bands: **(Fig. 9-31)**

a. Apply a thin bead of glue to one side of a piece of the red material.
b. Wrap the material around the lower end of the feather so that it meets in the back center of the feather.
c. Pinch the excess material together as in the diagram.
d. After 5-10 minutes, cut off the excess material. The result should be that the edges of the cloth meet and lay flush.
e. Use a whipstitch to sew up the cloth seam.
f. As you can see, this Option – with the exception of sewing up the back seam – can also be used to prepare feathers for the wrapping of thread bands.
4. Finish all the feathers with red base material and thread bands, if desired.

TIP DECORATIONS

Tip decorations should be applied after the above steps are completed. You can apply plumes only, hair tassels only, or both. With any of these, it is nice to have a "spot" at the bottom. **(See Figs. 9-29 & 9-30)**

Tip Plumes

Tip plumes will add a nice extra touch of color to your bonnet. If you want both tip plumes and horsehair adornments on the feathers, the hair must be applied before the plumes.

Horse Hair

1. Lay the feather on a protected work surface with the glossy (front) side up. Cover the bottom half with a book so as to weigh it down and keep it steady. (You may do several feathers at once by placing their ends under one book.)

2. Hold a bunch of horsehair (the amount you want on one feather) between your thumb and forefinger of the left hand near one end of the bunch. Tamp the hair ends to get them even, as much as possible. Then trim the end of that bunch even with sharp scissors.

3. While still holding the hair bunch, place a ½" long strip of glue at the top of the feather. Then carefully lay the clipped end of the hair bunch on the glue and gently press the hair down so that all the hairs make contact with glue. **(Fig. 9-32 & 9-33)**

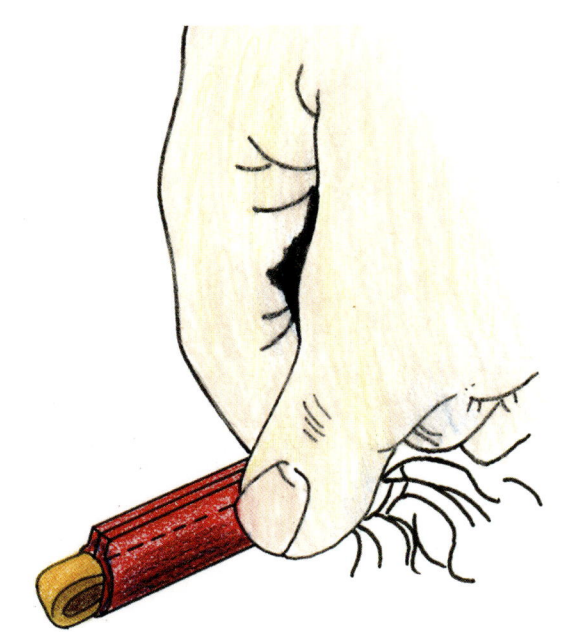
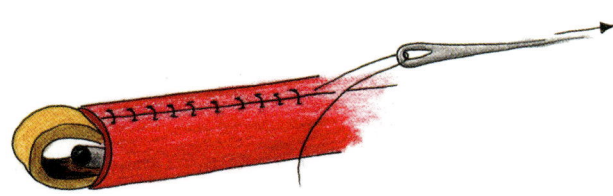

Fig. 9-31

Fig. 9-32

Fig. 9-33

4. While still holding the hair in position, place any kind of weight (e.g., another book) on the hair bunch above the glue so as to hold the hair firmly.

5. Apply horsehair to all the feathers and allow the glue to completely dry.

TIP PLUMES AND/OR OTHER DECORATIONS

As described in the Historical Section of this booklet, there are a variety of options for tip decorations. These include tip plumes, patches of rabbit or ermine fur, a circular piece of white tape or buckskin, a dab of white clay, etc. If you chose to use any of these methods, apply the decorations now over the glued end of the horsehair.

Tip Plumes

Tip plumes are usually short, no more than 2", and they generally have a backward curve, plus a "mini fluff" on the back. If you already have short fluffs, first pull off the "mini fluff". With larger fluffs, simply clip off the extra length of fluff and quill at the bottom to make a 2" tip plume; this also will remove the mini-fluff. **(Fig. 9-34)**

Fig. 9-34

If the fluffs have any backward curve, use your fingernail to gently crimp the plume so that it is straight and flat. Now, apply a tiny drop of glue on the clipped end of the glued horsehair and press the bottom of the tip plume into the glue so that it covers the end of the horsehair. **(Fig. 9-35)** Allow to dry. (If you have not already noticed, white craft glue dries clear, so it will not be apparent.) **(Fig. 9-36)**

"Spots"

If accent pieces of fur (cut into dots, squares, rectangles, etc.) are to be used – either on the feather tips or on the body of the feather, as in Figure 7-27a - mark the desired shape on the leather side of the fur. (Craft tip: Make a pattern of thin cardboard and trace around it.) If the shape is a square or rectangle, orient the long axis of this design so that it is parallel to the direction of the hair. Then carefully cut the piece out of the hide with a craft knife or razor blade, but do not cut hair on the other side as you cut through the leather. This will give the finished "spot" a nice, natural look by not having the hair chopped off around the edges.

Cut out all the pieces. If using horsehair but no plume, glue one spot to each feather so that it covers the clipped end of the horsehair and allow it to dry.

If the feathers have both horsehair and plumes (or plumes only), glue on a spot so that just the bottom end of the plume is covered.

Gypsum: An Alternative "Spot"

As discussed earlier, an authentic, historic method of tip decoration is to apply various types of white paste over the end of the horsehair tassel. **(See Fig. 7-24)** Contemporary bonnet maker Bill Brewer uses the following method: Buy powdered gypsum at the hardware store. As soon as you glue the horsehair to the feather tip, liberally sprinkle on the gypsum and very gently press it into the glue. When the glue is dry, simply blow the excess dust off of the feather.

"Double Tips" Decorations

If you really want to fancy up your warbonnet, you also can decorate the insides of the feather tips. On the back of each feather, simply glue on another tip plume and place a spot identically to the way the front of the feather is decorated. It is not necessary to add horsehair, as the hair tassel is readily visible from both the front and back sides of the bonnet.

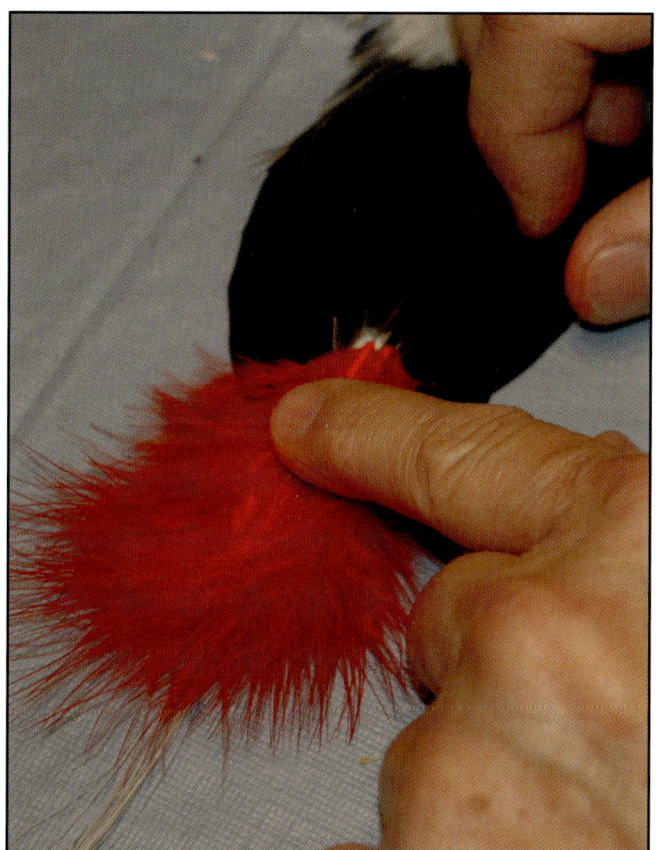

Fig. 9-35

Fig. 9-36

Note that the tip plume completely covers the end of the horsehair.

Pompon

This is an optional item which can be used in place of a front center feather. Components are not included in the Materials list at the beginning of this chapter. **(See Fig. 7-33)**

To begin construction, a stripped wing spike quill (or stick/dowel) the same length as the front center eagle feathers is readied. To use a quill, start with an extra-long spike, then cut off the thin, weak tip of the quill down to a thickness that will support the weight and movement of the hackles. (Note: In most of the examples the quill/stick is straight, especially in the Blackfoot Straight Up bonnets. However, in some of the Sioux examples, the quill has a slight backward curve like the other front feathers in the bonnet.) Rooster hackles in two different colors, red or black, have been seen on museum specimens, with red being the most frequently used. Today, craftsmen can buy hackles that are sewn together and sold as "strung saddle hackles". A string of these would be easiest to use, although hackles can be tied on individually if that is all that is available to the craftsman. We recommend 5" – 6" hackles.

Before tying hackles to the quill, pierce the quill for the secondary lace. Further prepare the quill by attaching a rawhide loop or making a self-loop in the quill end. (Some Straight Up Bonnet examples have no loop; rather, the end of the quill is left bare, and the completed pompon is firmly stitched at its bottom end to the center of the bonnet's head band.)

Begin by tying the start of the hackle string approximately 2" from the top of the quill, then tightly wind the hackle string downward and around the quill until you reach 1" or less from the end of the quill. As you go, orientate the hackles so that they flare outward like the photographic examples. Cut off the excess of the hackle strand, then tightly bind the base of those end hackles to the large quill. Now apply a wool fabric wrap (firecracker) that covers both the end of the hackles and top of the feather loop.

Major Plume

There is an endless number of ways the wing spike can be altered and decorated. (An alternative is to use a slender wood dowel.) **(Fig. 9-37)** For spikes, the basic feather is clipped off at the top, down to a thicker portion of the quill which is able to bear the weight of the tip adornments. Then, sections of webbing are sometimes trimmed or clipped so that the webbing itself in those areas becomes decorative. **(Fig. 9-38)**

Fig. 9-37 Photo by Joe Rosenthal
The webbing on this major plume wing spike has been completely stripped except at the tip.

Fig. 9-38
Webbing on front was trimmed with scissors for a sawtooth effect. Webbing on back side was partially stripped.

In addition, webbing can be removed completely from sections so that the bare quill at those points can be wrapped with strung beads, fur pieces, etc. **(Fig. 9-39)** Usually, large "breath plumes" are tied to the tip end, as well as strips of thin ribbon or yarn.

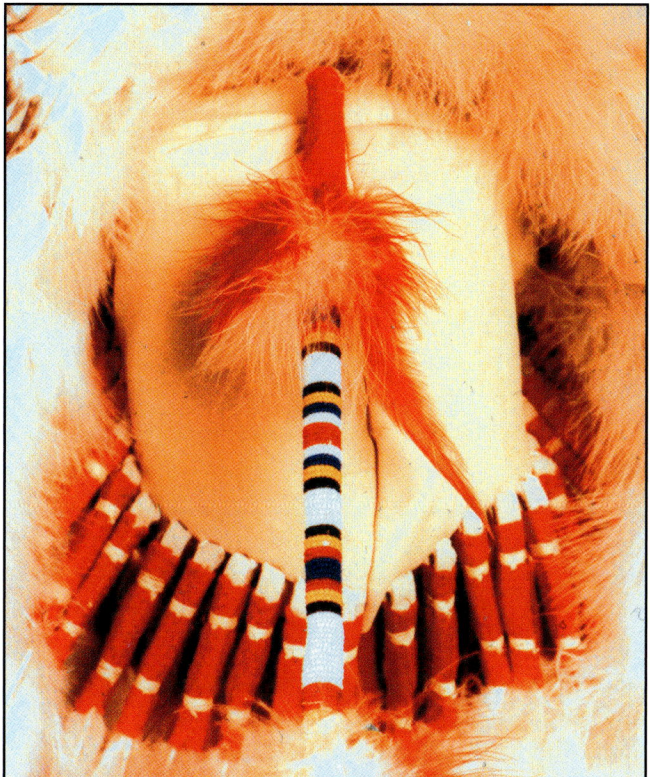

Fig. 9-39 *CCTP Photos*

The webbing has been entirely removed from the wing spike or dowel used for this major plume. Next, a thin layer of leather was glued to the section to be beaded. Beads were applied in a wrapped style, tacking the thread to the leather every 2-3 wraps to help secure the beadwork.

Note: If you use a wood dowel, it can be decorated similarly, but it should be covered completely with yarn, bead wraps, etc. so that none of the wood remains exposed.

Modern "major plumes" are constructed from a turkey wing spike that first has been straightened, and then a leather loop with red wool covering is attached like the other bonnet feathers. (Note that the loop is positioned on the sides of the quill instead of front and back.) An older alternative method of attachment is to make a self loop on the thick end of the quill. **(See Fig. 7-9)** Once it is attached to the crown, the major plume is free to swing and move, thereby adding grace to the already attractive sway of the bonnet itself.

BONNET ASSEMBLY

Feather Slits

The task of measuring for the feather slits on the crown is a bit tedious, but it is important so that the feathers will be uniformly spaced on both sides of the crown. Excellent results are achieved when the feathers are spaced the same distance apart from front to back. Because there may be some trail-and-error in this process, we recommend you make a paper pattern the same size as the crown and first use it to measure and mark lacing slits until you are satisfied with the spacing of the slits. If you do not use a pattern, you may end up with lots of confusing marks on your actual bonnet crown.

First, the crown must be completed as far as described at the beginning of the Construction instructions. Next, consider how many feathers you have (not counting the Major Plume). Of course, if you have a Center Feather, the first pair of slits will be centered directly above the center of the brow band.

Now you must measure the distance around one side of the crown. The slits should be ½" above the brow band and, further around, ½" from the bottom edge of the crown. **(See Fig. 9-40)** We suggest you use tailor's chalk and draw a line along these landmarks. Then begin measuring by starting at the center above the brow band, following the brow band to its end, angling past the outline for the medallions (or end of the brow band) down to about ½" above the edge of the crown, then on around to the back center of the crown. It is possible to do this with a cloth measuring tape, or use a non-stretchy cord of some sort and measure the distance you find by using the cord like a measuring tape around the crown.

Dividing this total length by the number of feathers on a side will tell you how far apart the slit pairs should be. For example, if the distance around one side of the crown is 13 ½", and you have 15 feathers on a side, divide 13 ½" by 15 to yield 0.9". Round this up, and the distance from one pair of slits to the next will be 1". (Actually, the marks you make will be the center point for the pair of slits, with one slit being on each side of the mark.) Since 15 feathers x 1" = 15" and your circumference is only 13 ½", we recommend spacing the feathers in the front of the bonnet ¾" apart, then spacing the feathers on back at 1" or so.

Fig. 9-40
For 1½" brow band, marks for slits are at 1¾". Note space for medallions at end of brow band.

This will require some trial and error. Remember that the distances you decide on will also be used to space the feathers on the other side of the bonnet.

If you have 31 feathers – which include a center feather - make a chalk mark at the front center ½" above the crown, then make another mark 3/4" from it and continue with dots at ¾" spaces but then graduating to 1" spaces after you get past the medallion area. The last pair of slits on each side should be 1/2" from the back center. (This way, the back two center feathers – one from the left side and one from the right - will be 1" apart.) Go back and count the number of slit pairs to make sure the number equals the number of feathers you have. If the number of slit pairs does NOT equal the number of feathers, you have made a mistake somewhere and need to either refigure your total distance, check your arithmetic, re-measure the slit pairs distances, or all three. In any case, you will have to re-measure and make new marks.

However, if you have an even number of feathers in the bonnet, consider that the front two center feathers will be a total of ¾" apart. Therefore, the first pair of slits above the brow band should be 3/8" from center, and the remainder will still be ¾" apart, etc. Again, the last pair of slits on the back center will be 1/2" from center.

Note: The tedious part comes from doing the arithmetic and arriving at a hard-to-measure distance between feathers (11/16", for example). In this situation, experiment with rounding the number to the next smaller one-eighth inch; in this case, 10/16" = 5/8". Here, you would space the feathers 5/8" apart from the front center and on around to a point on the crown somewhere after you go past the end of the brow band and onto the edge of the crown. From that point, you can re-measure and divide by the remaining number of feathers and find a comfortable spacing for the remaining feathers. This will probably mean that, like the example above, these back feathers are a little bit further apart than the ones on front, but this will not be noticeable in the completed bonnet.

Once you have determined the slit spacing for one side of the bonnet, it will be easy to measure and mark the other side. **(Fig. 9-40)**

Cutting Slits

Each of the two slits in a pair of lacing slits should be 1/4" apart and no longer than ¼". Ideally, the slits are just long enough for the lacing to pass through snugly. Find the first mark in the front center, then cut a slit on either side of it so that the 2 slits are ¼" apart and no longer than ¼" in length. We recommend that you use a craft knife or very sharp pen knife to make these cuts. Place a block of scrap wood inside the crown and cut through the crown material into the wood. By using the wood, you will be much less likely to make an error and cut a big slit, when you only intended to make it ¼" long. Cut all the slits for each side.

Finishing The Crown

In the Historical Section, we discussed various ways of covering the crown. This includes covering the entire crown with colorful material, sewing on strips of fur, or sewing on small plumes or body feathers. After the crown slits are cut – but before the feathers are laced on – is a good time to finish these crown decorations. You also should locate the position for attachment of the Major Plume and make slits in the top of the crown for its loop attachment. But do not tie on the Major Plume at this time.

If you wish to stitch on fluffies, select those which have a thick quill tip. Most of the quill tips of small fluffs are flimsy and eventually will split and pull off.

If you use secondary wing feathers, their quill ends should be big and strong enough to cut and make self-loops. It is best to start with a full-sized feather and cut the webbed tip off so that the finished feather (after the quill is made) is 4"-6". This allows for the full use of the "hollow" end of the quill to make a self-loop.

Stripped quill feathers were popular for crown decorations and are fun to make. The accompanying photo series shows this technique. **(Fig. 9-41 a thru f)** First, select 2-3 dozen secondary wing or tail feathers approximately 6" long (or, on longer feathers, cut the feather tips off square so that the entire feather is approximately 6"). Next, strip the webbing from top to bottom, as follows: With the front of the feather facing you, grab the webbing at the top and as close as possible to the quill on either side with both hands. While holding the feather steady with the left hand, carefully begin to pull the webbing down the quill with the right hand. Pull in short increments. The webbing should all stay in one piece, held together by the thin strip of tissue that attached the bottom of the webbing to the quill. Strip the webbing down to within 1" of the bottom of the webbing. Now, use your left hand and strip down the webbing on the opposite side. When the webbing has been stripped on both sides, simply cut off the bare quill just above the loose webbing.

Fig. 9-41f
Completed stripped feather with upper portion of quill removed.

After all your feathers are prepared in this manner, use Rit (TM) dye to dye the feathers an appropriate color, if desired. Be sure to dye the feather after stripping the web, so that the exposed quill area also is dyed. Set the dye with vinegar, as per the dye instructions, then rinse thoroughly until the water is clear. Pat the feathers fairly dry, then allow them to dry completely by laying them out on newspaper.

Now cut self-loops in the ends of the quills, as illustrated. **(Fig. 9-42)**

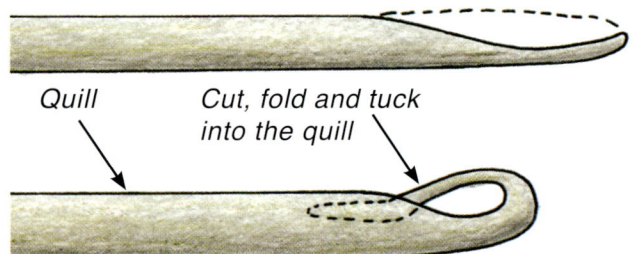

Fig. 9-42

To attach the feathers to the crown, first otherwise complete the warbonnet, then untie the eagle feathers at the back center. This will allow you to lay the tail feathers away from the bonnet for greater accessibility to the back of the crown.

To cover the crown with small trim feathers, start about 4" above the bottom of the crown and stitch or lace on a row of feathers. Add another row 3"-4" above the first, and so on, until you have covered the top and back of the crown. The finished effect will be somewhat like having a feather duster on the crown. **(Fig. 9-43)**

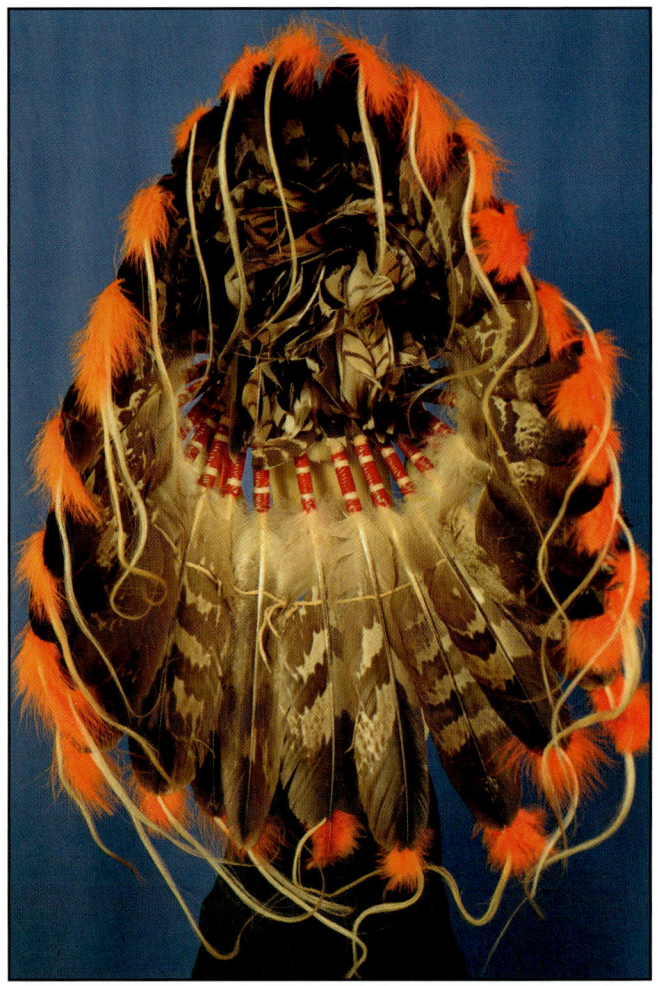

Fig. 9-43 *Courtesy of the Wagner Museum, Germany.*

A quick, modern way to cover a crown is to use small 2" fluffies. These are simply glued on one at a time, and this can best be done before lacing the eagle feathers to the bonnet. Glue these on by placing a drop of glue on the front of the fluff (as opposed to the inward curved back side). This way, the fluffs will curve out and away from the crown. NOTE: Do not place them closer than 2" from the slits where the eagle feathers are to be mounted. For the best effect, attach the fluffs in rows, with a slight overlap, similar to shingles on a roof. Start along the bottom and work up. These can cover the entire crown or merely the top and back.

If you plan to add a Major Plume, leave space for it and add it before tying the warbonnet back together.

Lacing On The Feathers

Select your Secondary Lace material at this time. Old Timers used a very thin piece of brain-tanned buckskin, as it is very strong, even when cut thin. A convenient material for Secondary Lacing is simulated sinew. If you use it, buy the full-thickness type. Also, a double thickness of kite string is a cheap substitute but probably will not last over the years. When unwaxed string or buckskin is passed through the hole in the quill, the feather will not slide freely once the feather is in position. However, when using simulated sinew, you should plan to go through the quill, then make a half-loop around the quill and go back through the same hole. **(Fig. 9-44)** This way, the half-loop can be pulled tight after the feather is in its proper position, and the feather will not slide out of place in the future. This method, while giving desirable results, is very tedious to work with when it comes time to lace up the feathers and then later adjust them.

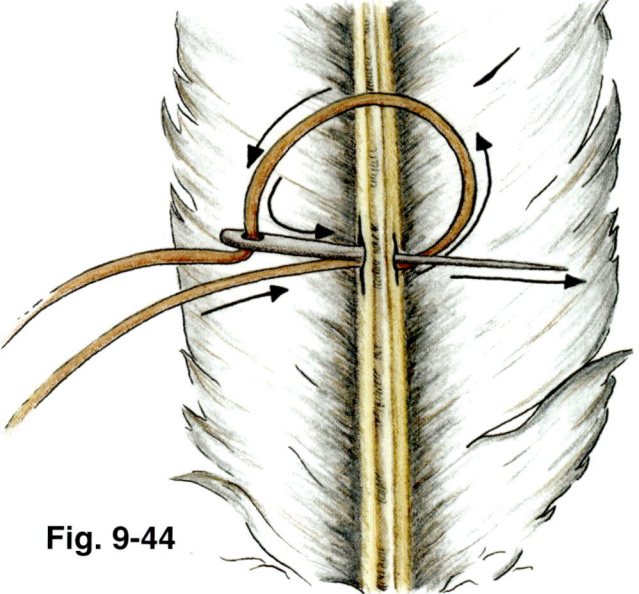

Fig. 9-44

The thong used to lace the feathers to the bonnet is called a Primary Lace. A very good Primary Lace can be made from buckskin, and even a standard leather boot lace will do. Buckskin is more supple, however, and will not cause the "buckling" of the crown between the slits like you will get with a thick boot lace. Of course, select a lace that is 1'-2' longer than the circumference of the crown.

1. Bring the lace through one of the front center slits until you have reached half its length. Then run it through the loop of the first feather and back into the adjacent slit. As you lace on the feathers, keep the lace straight so that it has no twists in it. Lace the feathers on somewhat loosely, as you can tighten them later. **(Fig. 9-45)**

Fig. 9-45

Lacing on the feathers. The left side of the bonnet has already been laced up.

2. Lace on all the Lefts, then go back to center and finish lacing on the Rights.

3. When you have done both sides, both ends of the lace will be on the underside of the bonnet. Simply tie them together with a loose knot, as you will retie and trim the ends later.

4. The Secondary Lace should be strung through the quill of each feather at this time. Use a large needle (e.g., a Darning Needle) and a pair of pliers to pull the needle through the hole you made in each quill 4" above the loop. This is a tedious task, as you must be very careful that the lace does not pull any of the fluffie into the lace hole. **(Fig. 9-46)**

Fig. 9-46

Sewing with the secondary lace. (Fluffs not shown). Note slight overlap of feathers on right.

5. Start at the front center and work toward the back. As you lace on each feather, position it so that it very slightly overlaps the feather next to it. In other words, the edge of the webbing that is on the side nearest to the brow band center should overlap some of the webbing of the feather next to it. After lacing on the last feather on the back of one side, do not tie off the lace but go back to the front center and lace on the feathers for the other side.

6. When all the feathers have been laced, the bonnet should appear as in this illustration. **(Fig. 9-47)** Now, bring the back center feathers together by joining the Secondary Lace ends with a loose knot. Do not cut off any excess Secondary Lace at this time.

7. Now go back and tighten the Primary Lace. Start at the front center and work back toward the end of the brow band. As the feathers descend around the end of the brow band toward the crown edge, the lacing should be loose so that the entire feather can fall back toward the back of the bonnet. When you reach the first feather at the edge of the crown, you can make the lacing a little tighter, just loose enough so that the feathers can move freely.

8. After adjusting the Primary Lace on both sides, tie the ends together with a square knot and clip off the ends, leaving a couple of inches from each lace.

9. Observe how the feathers fall. It is helpful to have someone seated who wears the bonnet while you make the final adjustments. With attention to the Secondary Lace, go back and adjust any feathers as necessary for all the feathers to be evenly spaced. Again, the feathers on the front half of the bonnet must be slightly overlapped. You may find that, for the bonnet to fall the way you want it to, you need to space the back feathers so that they barely touch, and this is perfectly okay.

10. Now for the "Wind Test". With the bonnet on someone's head, see if you can take your hands and make the feather circle collapse on all sides so that the feathers all point to the ground. If you can do this, then this is the look you will have when a big gust of wind blows the bonnet down over your head. When you can do this to your feathers, the Secondary Lacing is too loose. Simply go back and readjust all your feathers so that they are closer together. Start with the feathers on the back half and adjust them first, then try the Wind Test, and adjust either the back or front feathers as necessary to prevent this potential problem.

11. When you are satisfied with the spacing of the feathers and, overall, how the bonnet looks, then you can permanently tie off the secondary lace and cut off the ends (again, leaving a couple of inches of loose ends).

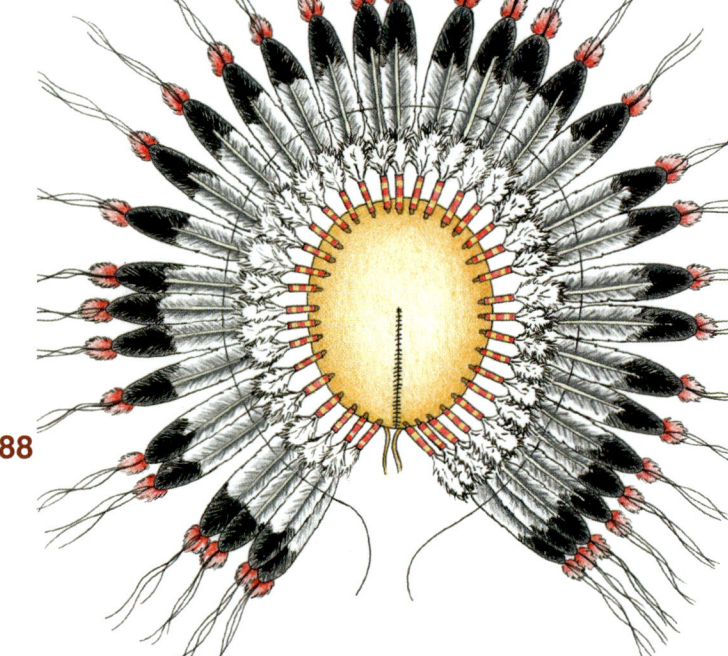

Fig. 9-47

This shows bonnet with primary and secondary laces in place, before final adjustments.

Attach The Major Plume

Remember that, earlier, you cut a pair of lacing slits in the top of the crown for the Major Plume. Use a thin, short thong and tie it into place. **(Fig. 9-48)** Tie it fairly snugly or else the Major Plume will flop around and end up sticking out of the side of your bonnet.

Fig. 9-48

Proper position for the Major Plume so that it does not fall too low and interfere with the bonnet feathers.

SIDE DROPS AND ROSETTES

See the Historical Section for the discussion on options for Side Drops. Contemporary fur strips are usually whole ermines or rabbit strips, while historic bonnets used ermine tubes.

White Rabbit Fur Drops

If you wish to use strips of rabbit fur, prepare them at this time. You will need:

    1. rabbit hide with white fur (with few or no holes)
    2. red wool or felt for "firecrackers" (optional)
    3. soft leather for lace attachments
    4. colored thread for "thread bands"
    5. Additional supplies: glue, needle, red thread (optional)

1. On the leather side of the hide, measure and use a pencil to draw the layout for the strips. The long dimension of the strip should run in the same direction as the

You can see that the strips will have various lengths after they are cut. They can be used this way or cut to a uniform length after cutting the strips from the hide. A minimum of four strips is needed, but you can use more if you like. It is also possible to sew two short strips together to make one long one, if necessary.

2. Use a single edge razor blade or Xacto knife to cut the strips. (We recommend that you cut the hide outdoors to avoid having rabbit fur all over your house.) The fur lies in one direction, so start at the "top" to make your cuts. Be careful NOT to cut the fur, just gently cut through the hide itself.

3. If you wish to have strips of the same length, determine that length, mark the strips, and cut them off at the "bottom" – again NOT cutting the hair. Thoroughly shake out all the strips and remaining hide before bringing them back inside.

4. For an economy bonnet, the strips can be sewn directly to the crown. Hold the top of a strip on the inside of the crown and use needle and thread to sew it to the crown. Usually, these strips are sewn on one at a time next to each other, not all together in one bunch. The edge of the first strip should be even with the end of the brow band. The use of thread similar in color to the color of the crown will make the stitches less obvious.

5. To make Fur Strip Drops, proceed as follows:
a. Cut a piece of red material 1 ½" x 2" for each fur drop. Lay out the red material so that the 2" dimension is up-and-down and the 1 ½" dimension is the width.

b. Trim the rabbit fur short at the top 1 ½" of the strip. Apply a thin layer of glue evenly with an artist's brush to the trimmed area and press that end of the strip onto the red material and directly in its center.

c. Cut leather laces approximately ¼" x 4". (Make at least ¼" wide, no thinner.)

Fig. 9-49

Partial rabbit hide showing pencil layout marks 1" apart on leather side of hide.

d. On the leather side of the fur strip, at the top, apply a line of glue approximately 1 ½" long down the center. Then press one end of the lace into the glue. The other end of the lace will extend out of the "firecracker" area approximately 2½".

e. Prepare all the strips as above and allow the glue to dry completely.

f. Now, start at one edge of the red material and roll it in on itself toward the other edge which should result in a red "firecracker".

g. While pinching the firecracker in one hand, take colored thread (usually white, yellow, or goldenrod) and wrap 1/4" wide thread bands around the material, with one band near the top and a second band near the bottom. Or you may use red thread to sew up the back of the firecracker and not use thread bands.

h. Complete all the drops as above. (Option: Instead of ending up with a single lace coming out of the "firecracker" that will be sewn to the edge of the crown, you can double the leather into a loop and glue both ends onto the fur. Drops made like this will, of course, require a separate thong and an awl to poke holes in the crown edge to facilitate lacing the individual drops in place.) **(Fig. 9-50)**

Ermine Tube Construction

Supplies Needed:

- Ermine hides (with or without heads or tails)
- Soft buckskin from which to cut thongs
- Piece of Black Bear or Skunk Fur (black)
- Red wool: 1 ½" H x 2" W (one for each tube)
- Heavy Colored Thread for firecracker wrap
- Alternate: Red sewing thread
- Craft Knife
- Scissors
- Ruler & Pencil
- Size 12 Sharps needles
- Size "D" Nymo (or smaller)
- Straight pins
- Spray bottle of rubbing alcohol
- Thick cardboard (12" x 12" or larger)

Ermine tubes are smaller, thinner versions of a case-skinned hide. They are the ermine drops most commonly seen on older bonnets, were used by many tribes, and they often were used on war shirts. **(Fig. 9-51)** The drawings in the Exhibit IX illustration set show the following construction steps: Each tube is made from a long narrow section of ermine hide having a faux ("fake") tail with black tip (using bear or skunk hair). The hide strip is

Fig. 9-50

Shows two options: (A) Lace made into a loop; (B) No thread bands on sewn material.

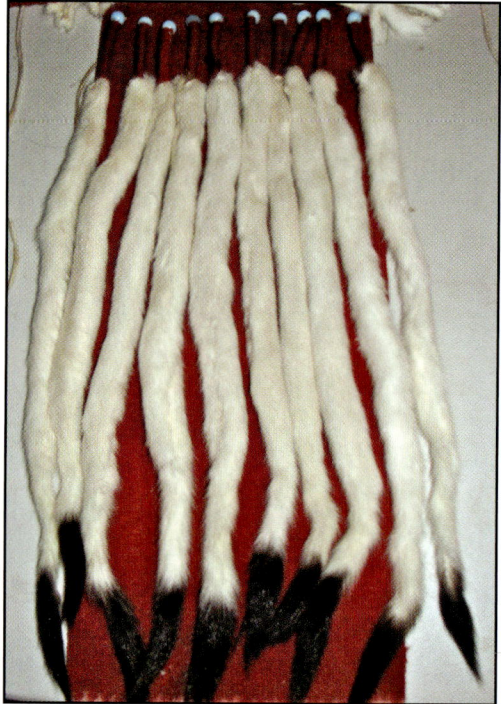

Photo by Allen Chronister

Fig. 9-51

Group of ermine tubes with firecrackers but no thread wraps. These are somewhat unusual in that each tube has an actual ermine tail.

sewn right-side-out into a tube, around a thick leather thong that runs the length of the hide strip plus 6" or so extending beyond the top which is used as a tie to attach the tube to the bonnet crown. To the other end of the thong is secured a tuft of black hair extending out of the bottom of the tube and which simulates the tip of an ermine's tail.

This technique of tube making uses ermine hides without heads or tails. If you have a hide with a tail, you can use the tail for at least one strip from the center of the hide. You can then use the faux tail method to make tubes from the remaining hide pieces or buy separate tails for each strip. However, most of the original ermine tubes had faux tails.

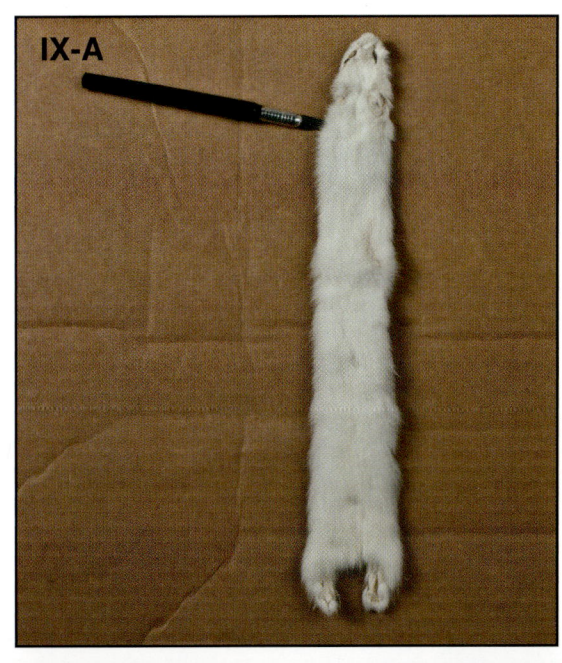

A single ermine hide usually yields 3-4 tube strips. You may use it with the head attached or choose to cut it off. If cased, slit the hide lengthwise down the center of the belly (or use a hide already split this way). **(IX-A)** Use a spray bottle filled with rubbing alcohol to completely dampen the inside of the hide. **(IX-B)** Next, pin the hide to a thick piece of cardboard, gently stretching it as much as reasonably possible to remove any wrinkles. **(IX-C)** The quickly evaporating alcohol allows the hide to dry in a short time.

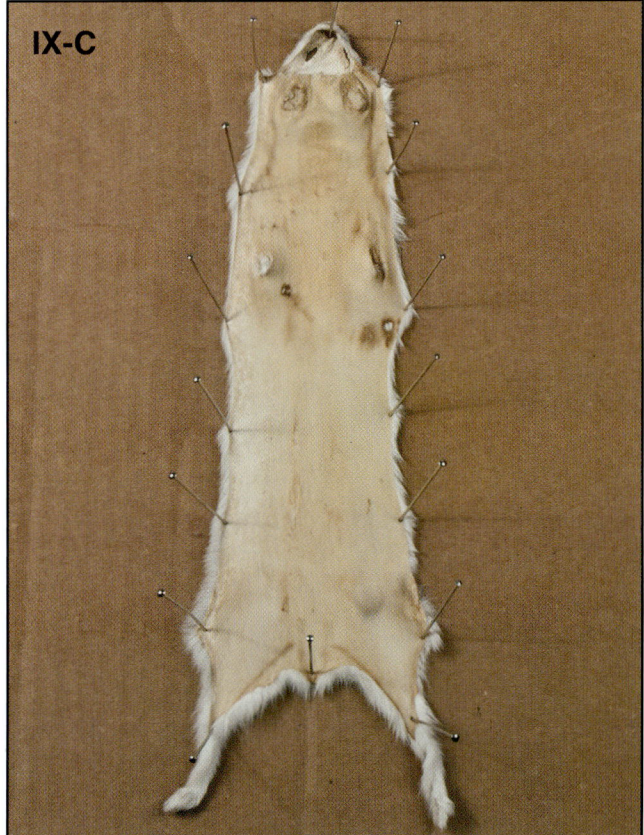

Remove the pins, then use a pencil to draw a line on the leather side from the center of the neck down to the center of the base of the tail. Measure across the hide at its narrowest point and divide by ½" to find out how many strips you can get from that hide. Using the center line as a reference, mark points across the bottom and top of the hide at ½" intervals, then connect the top and bottom marks. **(IX-D)**

Next, use an Xacto® knife or single-edged razor blade to cut out the strips. Start at the head end and slowly cut toward the tail. Lift up the top of the hide with your left hand as you cut with your right so that the hide is not laying flat on a surface. This will prevent your cutting the actual fur. After all the strips are cut, measure the shortest and cut the other strips to that length (again, just cut the hide and not the fur). Or you may determine that you wish to hang the drops from the bonnet graduating from the shortest at the side to the longest drops toward the back, etc. Also, if you have some short strips, you can carefully sew 2 pieces together to make a longer strip. (See Sewing information in the following paragraphs.) Use your imagination to make as many strips as you need and to make the most of the materials at hand.

Ermine Tube Components

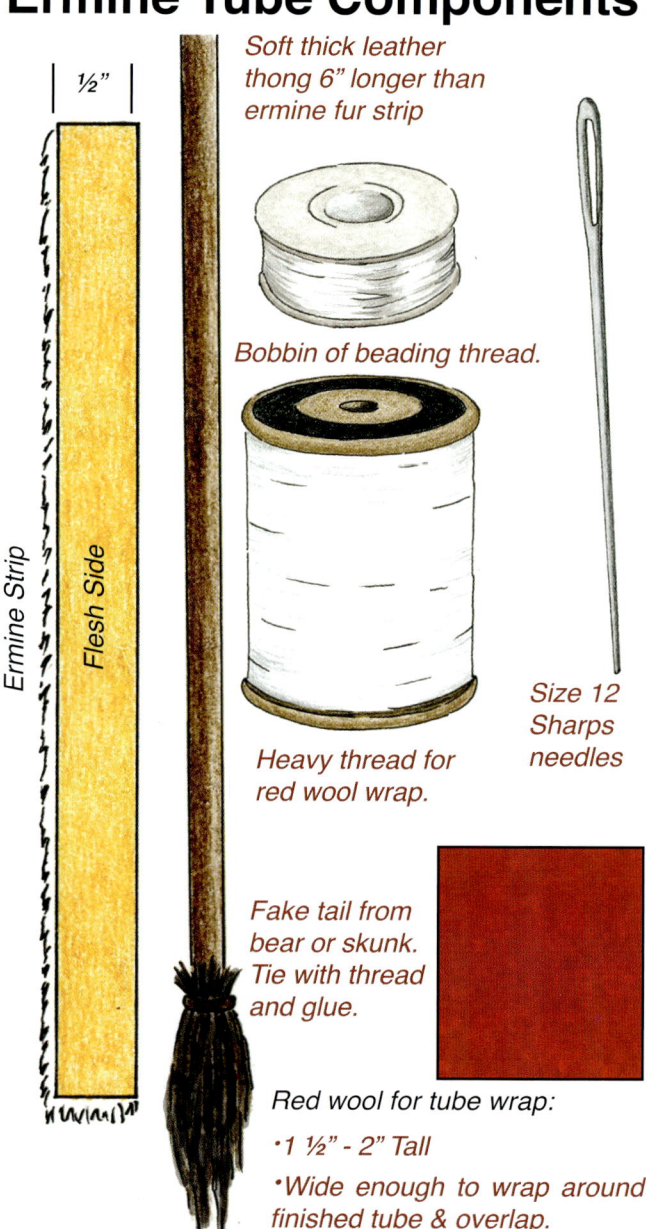

½"

Ermine Strip

Flesh Side

Soft thick leather thong 6" longer than ermine fur strip

Bobbin of beading thread.

Heavy thread for red wool wrap.

Size 12 Sharps needles

Fake tail from bear or skunk. Tie with thread and glue.

Red wool for tube wrap:
- 1 ½" - 2" Tall
- Wide enough to wrap around finished tube & overlap.

(See IX-E) Now cut a thick, soft leather thong that is ~6" longer than the hide strip for which it will be used and stretch it out. It forms the core around which the ermine tube will be sewn. However, the thong should not be so thick that it completely fills the inside of the tube, as this will make it tedious to sew up the tube.

Next, create the black tail tip approximately ¾" – 1" long. This requires the use of black bear or skunk fur. (Rabbit hair is too fine and too short, and horse tail hair is too coarse.) Tie a knot with thread to anchor the thread to the end of the thong, then carefully wrap on a sprig of hair. Too much hair looks inappropriate, so experiment to find just how much hair you need to make the tip look natural. When satisfied, you can apply a drop of craft glue to the thread wrap and allow it to dry. If necessary, you can shape the "tail tip" by trimming the sprig of hairs with sharp scissors, but do not overdo this or it will not look natural.

The next step is to sew the hide strip into a tube with the thong inside. **(IX-F)** Because ermine hide is so thin, we suggest using a Sharps needle and size D or smaller thread (smaller is better). Use the single thread method (as opposed to doubled thread). Position the thong so that the thread section of the hair tip is just above the bottom end of the fur strip. Start sewing at the "head" end of the strip and include some stitches to secure the thong inside the hide tube. Use a baseball stitch and gently sew the hide lengthwise with stitches 1/4" to 3/8" apart. As you tighten the thread, work to avoid pulling ermine hair into the stitches. We suggest making three or four loose stitches, tightening the first two, then making more stitches, etc. It is much more tedious to tighten each stitch as you go. Except at the start of your sewing, do not attempt to have the stitches catch the leather thong, as it merely hangs loosely inside the tube.

Tip: After stitching the thong to the top of the hide tube, place a heavy weight on the free end of the thong. This will provide some resistance to work against as you manipulate and sew the tube. Finish sewing up the tube.

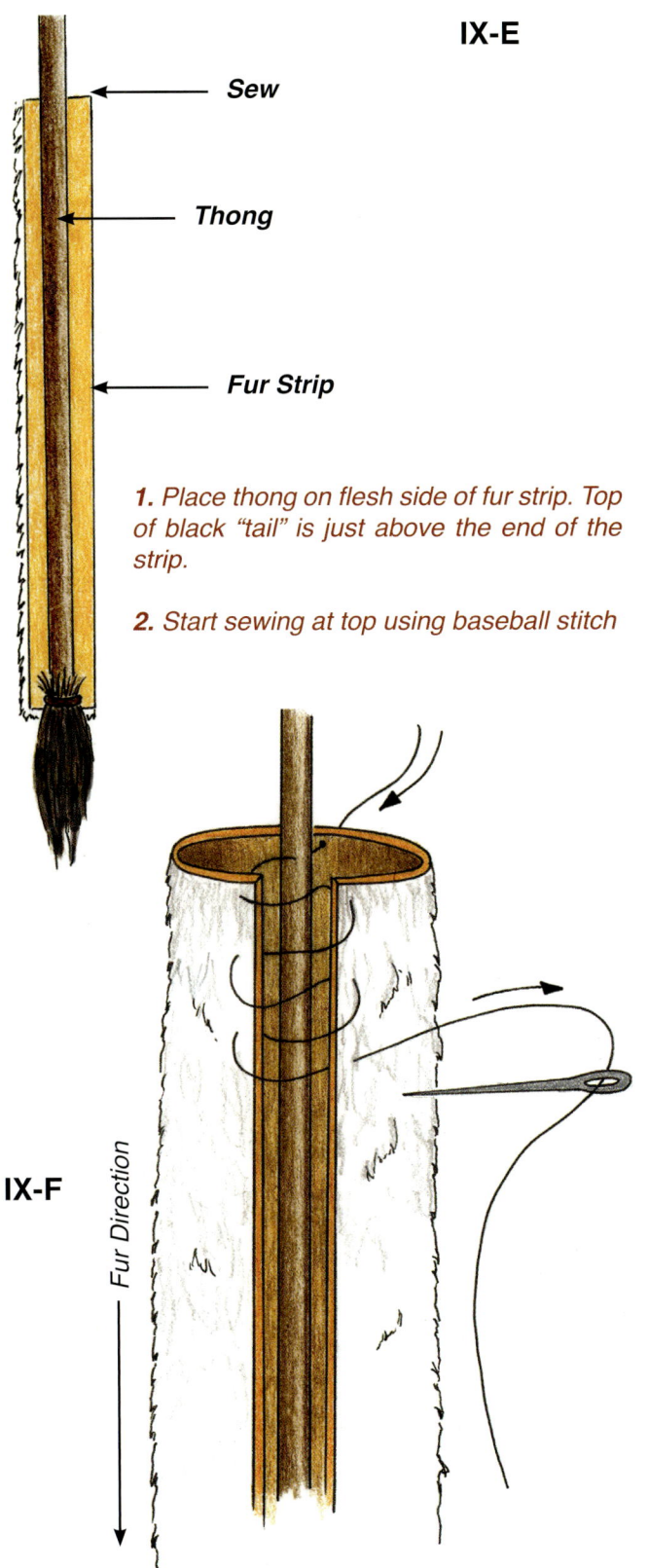

IX-E

1. Place thong on flesh side of fur strip. Top of black "tail" is just above the end of the strip.

2. Start sewing at top using baseball stitch

IX-F

Start sewing at top by securing thong to hide. Use baseball stitch. Make stitches 1/4"-3/8" apart.

After the tubes are completed, prepare red wool wraps for the firecracker section at the tops and apply them as you did the wraps for the bonnet feathers. Attaching the tubes to the bonnet is simply a matter of using an awl to poke holes along the edge of the crown, then inserting the thong end from the outside and tying two adjacent ties together on the inside of the crown.

Attaching Side Drops

If you use ribbons, rabbit fur drops, real ermine tube drops, or similar materials, they should be attached at this time. As per the above instructions, they usually are not attached in clusters but, rather, side by side from the brow band on back. Sew the drops to the inside of the crown. For fur drops with a single lace that extends from their tops, the laces can be sewn to the crown, or a hole can be poked above the edge of the crown. Poke the lace through the hole and tie a knot a knot in it or tie it to the lace of the drop next to it. Leave enough slack so that the drop can dangle freely.

Attaching Medallions

Remember that, after you sewed on the brow band, you positioned the medallions so they overlapped the ends of the brow band, then drew a pencil line around the medallion edge where it overlapped onto the crown. **(Fig. 9-52)**

Place one medallion in position, then begin sewing the medallion to the crown with needle and thread. Use a small sewing needle and doubled thread that is the same color as the background color of the beadwork. If part of the medallion extends beyond the edge of the crown, then you will only sew around the upper portion; you do not need to sew across the lower portion of the medallion to secure it to the bottom edge of the crown. Make running stitches between the 2nd and 3rd row of beads. (Whipstitching around the edge of the beadwork looks messy.) The portion of the stitch that is on the bead side needs only be 1/16" of an inch or so, and then on the inside of the crown go ¼" or so to make the next stitch. This way, there is very little thread on the beaded side, and it is less likely to show.

Option: For quilled wheels or quilled medallions, mirrors, etc., these do not need to (or cannot) be sewn to the crown. Instead, use an awl to pierce the **backing** of the mirror (first remove the mirror itself) or medallion with two adjacent holes near the center and run a 4" or longer thin thong through them. (Use a big needle for the leather backing on the medallion.) Then poke corresponding holes next to the end of the brow band, run the laces through those holes, and tie them together with a square knot on the inside of the crown. Beaded medallions can also be attached in this manner, but they tend not to look as good as ones that are sewn on.

It's Done

So, now you're done! But, is any project ever really finished? You may make changes, deletions, or additions to the drops on your bonnet. Or you may wear it awhile, then decide to adjust the feathers so that the bonnet lays or falls differently. Nevertheless, please consider your warbonnet as a living thing and treat it with the respect it deserves. Not only will the bonnet last indefinitely, but, in this way, you will be giving proper respect to its historic significance and the warriors of old. After all, your bonnet represents a REAL warbonnet. **(Fig. 9-53)**

Fig. 9-53

WaNonSheZhinGa, Ponca, wears a Stand Out style single trailer warbonnet with an atypical brow band design. The bonnet has no rosettes and uses eagle tail feathers and ermines as side drops. In this early 1900s photo, he also wears a Southern Plains style of buckskin shirt, along with a German silver tie slide. Early photos of Poncas wearing warbonnets are fairly rare.

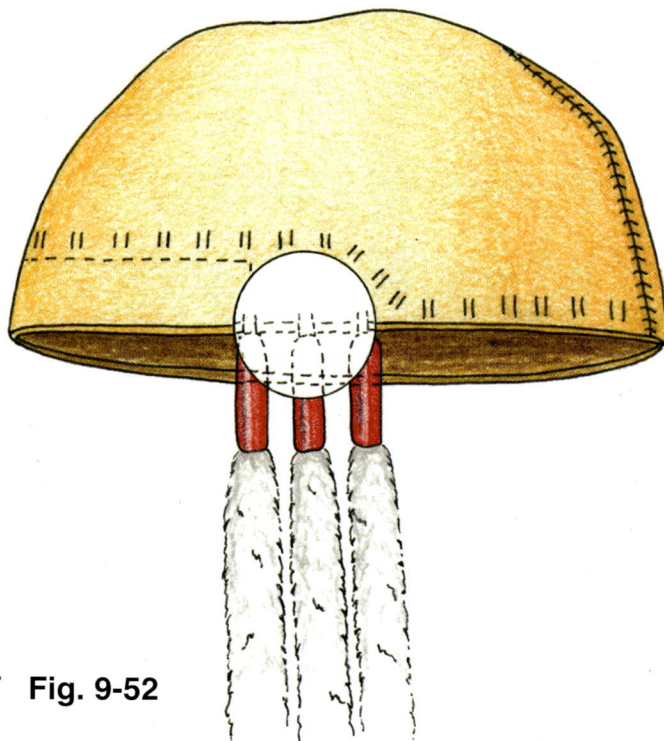

Fig. 9-52

Medallion overlaps end of brow band and partly extends below edge of crown in this example.

Wisconsin Historical Society 27991.

Fig. 10-1

Shoshone Double Trailer Horned Bonnet, ca. 1915.

Buffalo Bill Historical Center, Cody, Wyoming, U.S.A.; Adolf Spohr Collection, Gift of Larry Sheerin, NA.205.3

Trailer Bonnets 10

A variation of the Plains warbonnet had either one or two streamers of feathers, referred to today as "trailers". **(Fig. 10-1)** As with any handmade item common to a number of tribes and constructed by individuals, there were numerous variations of techniques for constructing trailers, attaching them to the bonnet crown feathers, then decorating the trailer. However, we will give you some basics to help you achieve either a Single or Double Trailer Warbonnet.

Materials

(Note: These are materials for the trailer only and do not include items needed to make the basic bonnet without a trailer as described in the previous chapter.)

A. 15 Imitation Eagle Tail Feathers for each Trailer. Feathers in each trailer should be all from the same wing side. For a single trailer, they can be either Lefts or Rights. For the Double Trailer, use all Lefts for one side and all Rights for the other. Also, you may determine that you want more than 15 feathers on your trailer(s). The quantities of supplies listed below assume the use of 15 feathers per Trailer.

B. 5" – 6" base plumes: 1 oz. for Single Trailer, 2 oz. for Double Trailer.

There should be an equal number on both the front and the back of each Tail Feather, either 2 or 3 plumes per side. The quantities above are enough so you can sort for the best fluffies in each ounce.

C. Tip Plumes: 1 oz.
Place a tip plume on each side of each feather.

D. Red wool (or wool felt) for Base Wraps (Firecrackers): 2 ½" x 24" - 1 piece for Single Trailer, 2 pieces for Double Trailer

E. Red* wool (or wool felt): 5" x 72" – Used for the Trailer itself. "Saved List" Trade Cloth is ideal.
*You may choose a different color than red; e.g. navy blue.

F. Calico* cloth: 1 piece 8" x 72" – Trailer Backing
* Calico is an inexpensive period-correct pattern. However, you may choose different period-correct material.

G. Leather for loops (stiff, such as thin rawhide) 1 piece 4" x 4 ½" (or 8" x 4 ½" for Double Trailer)

H. Horsehair: ¼ - ½ oz. of 12" – 14" hair. Color should be the same as that used in the main bonnet.

I. 48" Leather lace, 1 per Trailer – Used as Primary Lace for attaching the feathers to the trailer.

J. 1 Bobbin of heavy cotton thread for colored thread bands on the Firecrackers (Same color of thread as used on the main warbonnet feathers.)

K. 6' Simulated Sinew or heavy string: 1 piece per Trailer for secondary lace.

CONSTRUCTION

Trailer Bonnets

SINGLE TRAILER bonnet construction is a rather simple matter of making a basic warbonnet, adding the trailer material, then lacing on the trailer feathers, and attaching the top end of their secondary lace to the secondary lace of the basic bonnet.

DOUBLE TRAILER use either of two construction techniques, as described in the Historical Section. For one method, we find that, instead of tying the crown feathers together in a circle, the trailer feathers on each side become a continuation of the bonnet feathers as they come off the crown. **(See Fig. 7-37)**. In the second style, the customary feather circle is created on the bonnet, then the two trailers of feathers are tied into the side feathers of the crown. **(See Fig. 7-38)**

FEATHER PREPARATION Prepare all the feathers as you did for the main warbonnet, using the instructions given previously. You may wish to make these trailer feathers only 12" and cut the wood dowel extenders accordingly.

Differences between the bonnet and trailer feathers have to do with the number and placement of the base and tip plumes. For trailer feathers, there should be one tip plume on each side of the tip of each feather, and, on the back of the feather, you should have duplication of any other tip decorations from the front, such as spots. Horsehair tassels only need to be applied to one side of the feather tip.

There should be an equal number of base plumes on both the front and back, with 2 as a minimum and 3 resulting in a full look.

CROWN CONSTRUCTION Refer to the instructions given earlier for making and decorating the crown. This includes sewing on the brow band but waiting to add the medallions and side drops. You should also apply any crown fluffies, material, or other decorations.

Feather Slits

SINGLE TRAILER For a single trailer bonnet with 30 crown feathers, mark the crown for all 30 feathers, just as you were instructed to do for a bonnet without trailer. Note: Be sure and leave enough room below the slits in the back to attach the cloth trailer. The bottoms of the feather slits should be a full ½" above the crown edge.

DOUBLE TRAILER If you prefer the style where trailers are attached to each side of a full circle of crown feathers, make the basic warbonnet, then proceed to the next step for attaching the trailer. If you wish to make the style where the trailers are continuations from each side of the crown, proceed as follows: Unlike the basic bonnet, make only 12 feathers for each side. The back portion of the crown will have no feathers. Then, from the center of the crown above the brow band, mark the crown for 12 slit pairs on each side, spaced ¾" apart. (Remember, the slits in a pair are ¼" apart, and each slit is no more than ¼" long.) Lace on the crown feathers with primary and secondary laces but do not tie the secondary laces together. Now, make and attach the trailer.

Trailer Bonnets

The wool trailer should be backed with calico (or an even heavier material) like that shown in **Fig. 10-2**. This backing gives extra body to the trailer, making it less likely to twist when being worn. In this example, the backing is folded back onto the front of the trailer and sewn so as to form a binding around the red trailer edges.

Double trailer panels are especially prone to fold together down the middle. One measure to add additional stiffness to the panel is to sew an extra layer of thick canvas between the wool and calico. (Occasional old examples have a large piece of rawhide either sewn into the panel or used as the panel itself, instead of a fabric panel.)

A further measure is a variation on the one piece panel. Some double trailers were actually split up the middle from the bottom to about half way up the material. This feature allowed each side of the trailer and its feathers to drape on either side of a horse as the warrior rode along. **(See Fig. 7-41)**

Fig. 10-2 (Next Page)
Warbonnet with detail photo showing trailer lacing.

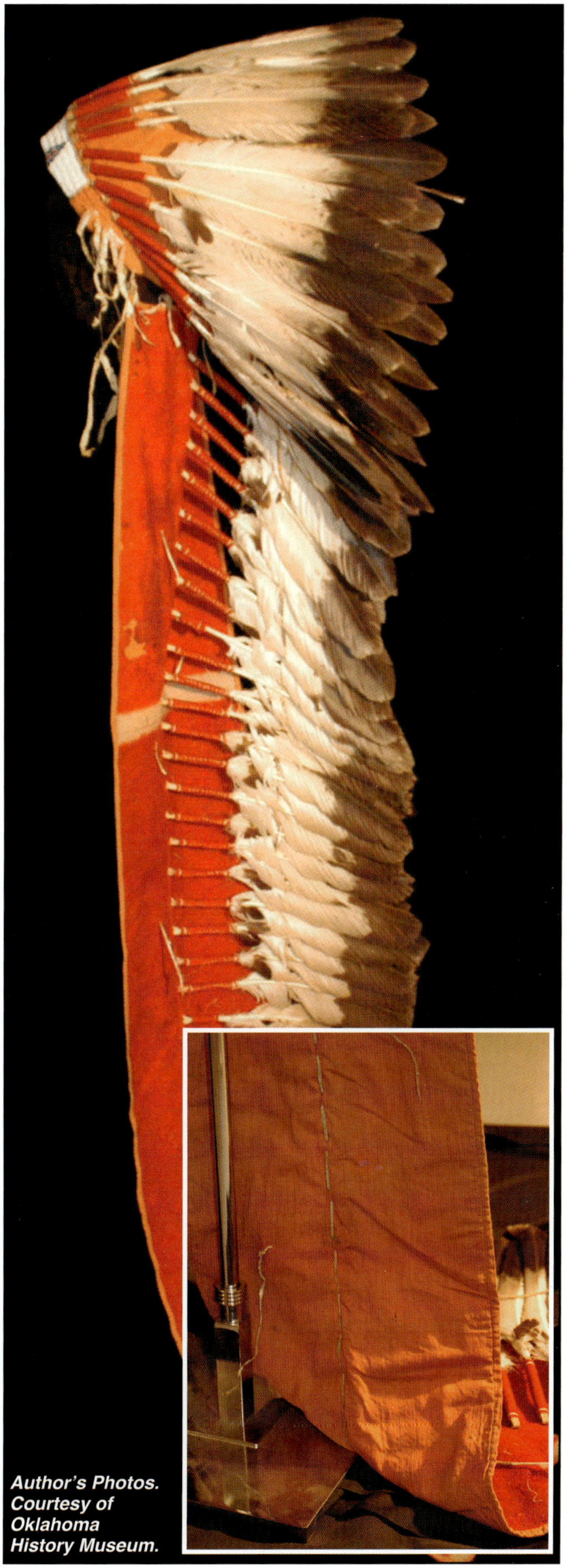

After the backing material is applied, attach the various trailer decorations. The kinds and forms of decorating were infinite in number, and they often reflected the personal taste, dreams, or power symbols of the wearer. Examples include bead lanes stitched horizontally across the trailer at spaced intervals, other beaded figures, hawk bells, feather clusters, single feathers, metal fringe sewn in horizontal rows, etc. **(Fig. 10-3)** We recommend that you decorate the panel at this time, with the exception of feather clusters which might get in the way as you attach the feather trailers.

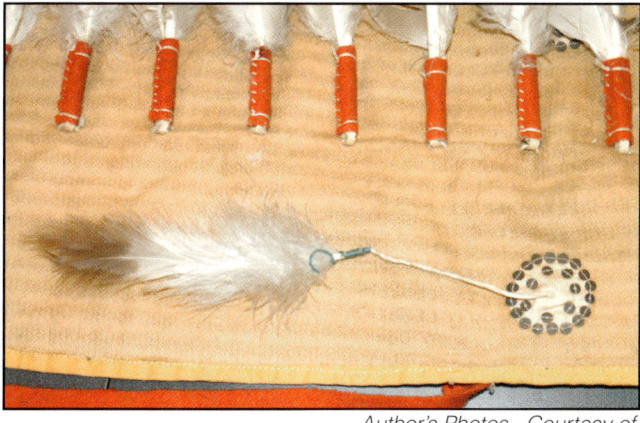

Author's Photos. Courtesy of Oklahoma History Museum.

Fig. 10-3

Detail of Southern Cheyenne Trailer. Brass sequins are sewn into a circle from which is suspended a "breath plume".

When finished, sew or lace the trailer to the crown. **(Fig. 10-4)**

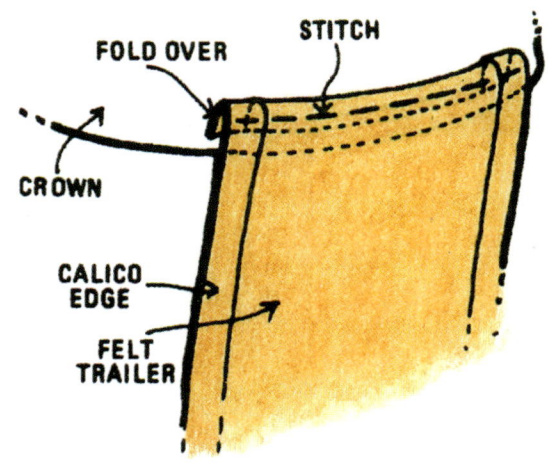

Fig. 10-4   *Sewing Trailer to Crown*

Also shown are 2 historic examples of old Cheyenne trailer bonnets. **(Fig. 10-5 & Fig. 10-6)**

Author's Photos. Courtesy of Oklahoma History Museum.

Fig. 10-5

Left: Detail image of a Southern Cheyenne war bonnet made using all wing spikes. This trailer has been attached to the crown with continuous stitching.

Author's Photos. Courtesy of Oklahoma History Museum.

Fig. 10-6

Right: Trailer was attached by "tacking" it to the crown at several places using thin leather laces.

Author's Photos. Courtesy of Oklahoma History Museum.

DOUBLE TRAILER Begin both of the two styles of Double Trailer bonnets the same. Lace the feathers with the Primary and Secondary Laces. Leave the Secondary Lace untied at the back. As noted in the previous paragraph, the feathers on the back sides of the bonnet should stand out, rather than lay down, and, thus, the back crown feathers should be more closely positioned on the secondary lace than a basic bonnet

MAJOR PLUME Now is a good time to attach the Major Plume to the bonnet crown. Remember to tie it snugly so that it swings very little from side to side. It also cannot droop downward when the bonnet is worn, as it will tangle with the other bonnet and trailer feathers.

Trailer Lacing

SINGLE TRAILER Mark the trailer for its feather slits. Actually, you should use an awl to poke holes, rather than slits. Starting at the top of the trailer and 1"- 2" from the crown edge, make a series of marks down the trailer center. A good distance to space the feathers is 2" apart. If you have 15 feathers in your trailer, then make 15 marks. You can then use the reference marks for poking pairs of holes for the Trailer primary lace.

Poke the holes of each pair ¼" apart and go all the way through both layers of cloth. Do not poke the second pair of holes until you have laced on the first feather, as the holes tend to "shrink" if not used immediately. Tie an overhand knot on one end of the primary lace, then cut a point on the other end and poke it through the first hole at the top from the under side. You may stiffen the lace point with a heavy application of beeswax.

Lace on the first feather so that its front edge points toward the crown, then poke the lace through the second hole. Now, poke the second pair of holes. Continue in this manner with the remaining trailer feathers, keeping all of them facing in the same direction. When you are finished lacing on the last feather, snug the lace up down the entire length of the trailer and tie off both ends with a knot. Do not pull the lace so tight that lumps are formed between the feathers. **(See Fig. 10-2)**

Now prepare the secondary lacing by threading it onto a very large needle. If using simulated sinew or string, thread it so that the lace is doubled. You can now start sewing the feathers together through their 4" holes by beginning at either the near or far end. You may find

Fig. 10-7 *Courtesy of the Wagner Museum, Germany.*

Crown Lacing

SINGLE TRAILER Follow the instructions in the previous chapter for lacing the crown feathers with the Primary and Secondary Laces. Do not tie off the ends of the Secondary Lace just yet. **NOTE:** The crown feathers in back should not lie down on your back when the bonnet is placed on your head. Rather, they need to stand out at a small angle. **(Fig. 10-7)** This will require you to position the feathers on the secondary lacing for the back half of the bonnet more closely than you would if this were a bonnet without a trailer. After you have adjusted the spacing for the feathers, tie off both the Primary and Secondary laces as for a finished bonnet..

it easiest to start at the last feather and tie a secure knot in the end of the lacing. **(Fig. 10-8a, b, & c)** As you string them together, carefully space them so they also are 2" apart. When all the trailer feathers are sewn with the secondary lace, tie the remaining end at the secondary lacing knot of the crown feathers, between the back-most Left and Right feathers.

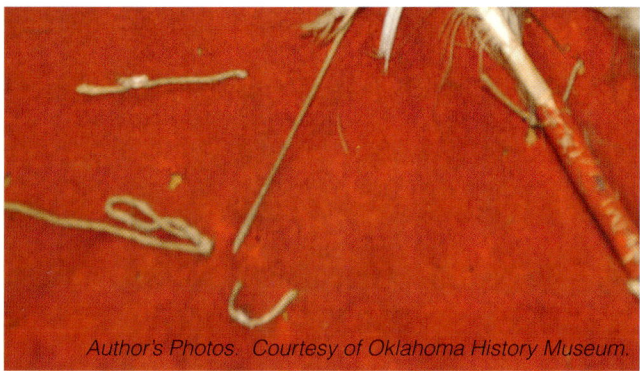

Fig. 10-8a
Secondary lace of this Cheyenne bonnet is anchored to the trailer with a simple stitch and knot.

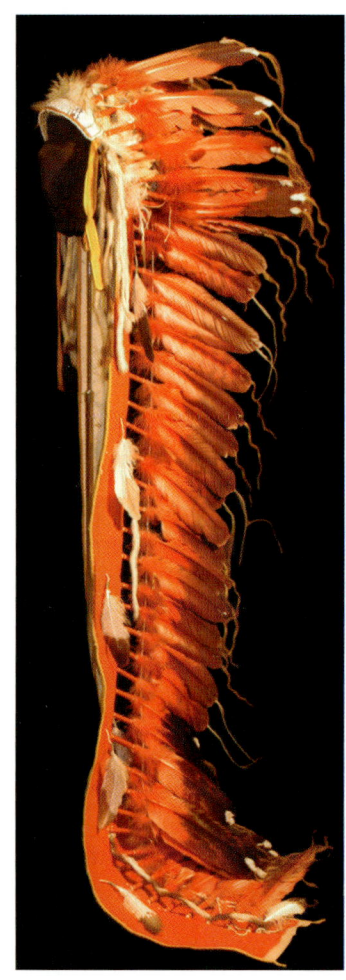

Fig. 10-8b   Author's Photos. Courtesy of Oklahoma History Museum.

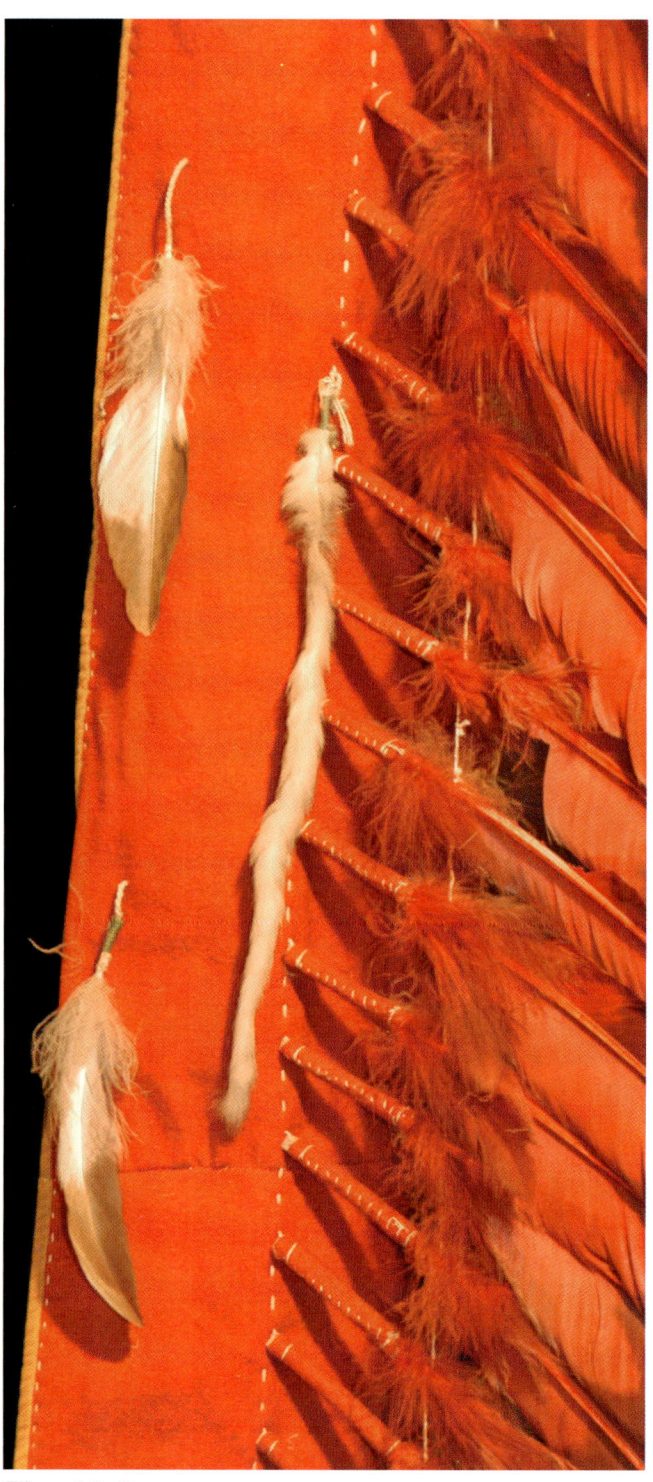

Fig. 10-8c   Author's Photos. Courtesy of Oklahoma History Museum.

The trailer from this extraordinary Cheyenne bonnet reveals how additional stitches were made with the primary lace through the material between each feather. This helps keep the primary lace taut. Notice, too, how tightly each feather loop is cinched down onto the trailer material. The entire bonnet is composed of dyed red immature golden eagle tail feathers and red fluffs.

DOUBLE TRAILER See Fig. 10-9 which illustrates the positions of the trailer feather holes for the Double Trailer Bonnet. Starting near the crown on each side, make reference marks down the trailer 2" apart for the holes placements. Then follow the above instructions for attaching the feathers with Primary Laces.

After the Trailer Feathers are attached with the Primary Lace, snug the lace up and tie off both ends with a knot. Do not pull the lace so tight that lumps are formed between the feathers.

Now, sew the feathers together using Secondary Laces as described in the Single Trailer bonnet. Start with the feather at the far end. When you have finished lacing on the top Trailer Feather and are satisfied with the spacing, tie the end of the Trailer Secondary Lace to the Crown Secondary Lace. For the style with the complete circle of crown feathers, tie onto the Secondary Lace between the crown feathers nearest to the side (3-4 feathers from the back center) so that the trailers will stay in a straight line when you are finished. For the bonnet style where the trailers are continuations of the crown feathers, simply tie to the Secondary Lace on either side of the back of the crown. In both styles, tie only a loose knot on each side, then have someone model the bonnet while you look at both sides to see if any additional feather adjustments need to be made on Secondary Laces. When you are satisfied, tie secure knots with these laces and trim off the ends.

Finishing Up

DROP AND TRAILER DECORATION Now is the time to add the side drops to the bonnet crown and any trailer decorations that still need to be done. See the discussion for basic bonnet construction regarding placement and attachment of the drops and medallions.

CHIN TIES You may also have found that, when this bonnet is worn, the weight of the trailer pulls the bonnet back on top of your head. In this case, you may add chin ties. Simply poke a hole under each medallion and run a 15"-18" lace with a single knotted end through the hole on each side, with the knot on the inside of the crown. These laces should be sufficient to keep the warbonnet in proper position on your head, especially when dancing or walking about.

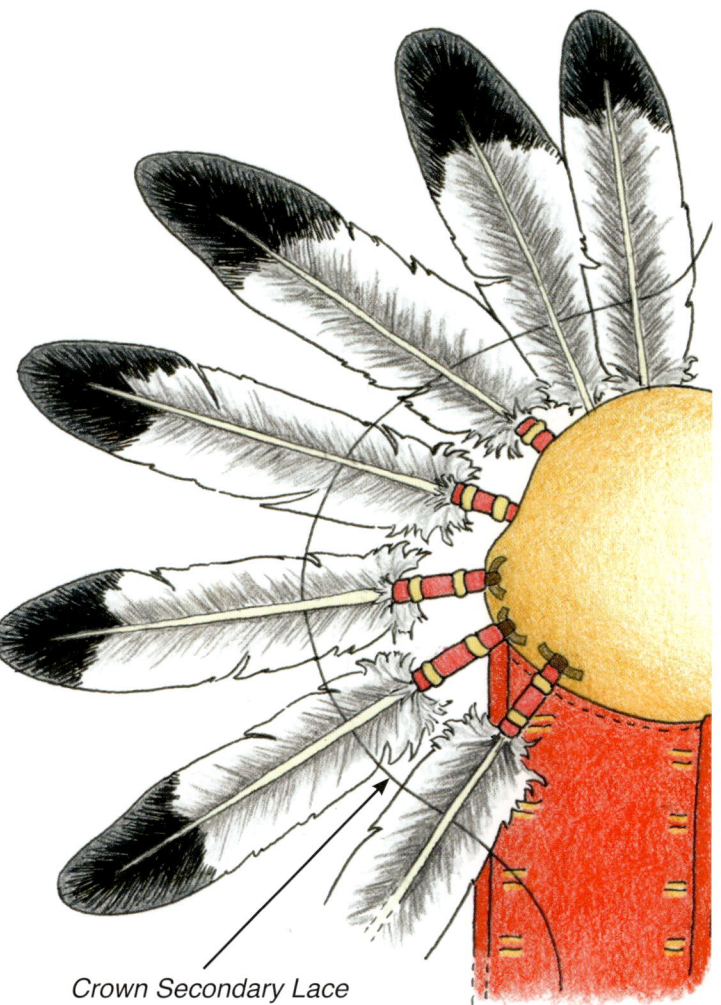

Crown Secondary Lace

Fig. 10-9
For both styles of double trailers, the crown feathers first must be strung with the crown secondary lace. In this example, the trailer feathers will be a continuation of the crown circle. Note that the last crown feather is in line with the feather slits on the left side of the trailer.

Fig. 11-1a

Fig. 11-1b

Fig. 11-1a & b

Blackfoot Straight Up Warbonnet. Instead of a crown, the foundation for this style of headdress is a wide rawhide brow band covered with red trade cloth. Materials used in this example include immature golden eagle tail feathers, dyed rooster hackles, ermine fur, horsehair, hawk bells, brass buttons, porcupine quills, and yarn.

Buffalo Bill Historical Center, Cody, Wyoming, U.S.A.; Chandler-Pohrt Collection, Gift of Mr. and Mrs. Richard A. Pohrt, Sr., NA.203.357

Straight Up Bonnets 11

As discussed earlier, the Straight Up bonnet **(Fig. 11-1)** has long been favored by the Blackfeet, Flathead, and other Plateau tribes. Evidence shows that this style pre-dates the adoption of the flared, Plains style bonnets which became popular with these tribes in the 1800s and continue to be so today. Among the Blackfeet, ownership of such a bonnet was reserved for certain men of status.

Examination of old photos and museum specimens reveals that, like Plains bonnets, there are variations in how the individual examples were constructed. However they bear similarities. The Straight Up bonnet consists of a wide rawhide strip that wraps around the wearer's head, and to it are attached a complete circle of eagle feathers. The bridal or secondary lace of the feathers is snugged to a degree such that they stand almost straight up, with only a slight flare. The rawhide head strap is covered with material – usually trade wool – and its ends join in the back where they are secured with a thong. As you can see in **Fig. 11-1b**, the ends of the trade wool hang loosely in the back. Oftentimes, a pompon of colored rooster hackles is positioned in the front center of the bonnet.

Following is a summary of how a typical example might be made, based primarily on photos of Mountain Chief, Blackfoot, and other members of his tribe. **(Fig. 11-2 & 11-3)**

Mathers Museum of World Cultures, Indiana University
Fig. 11-2

Mountain Chief (Ninastoko), 1848-1942, Blackfoot. Photo by Joseph Dixon, ca. 1913. The last hereditary Blackfoot chief. He wears a Straight Up bonnet with a slight flare, a pompon in the center, 3 rows of small brass buttons (?), fringed ermine hides, and a large number of ermine tubes.

Mathers Museum of World Cultures, Indiana University

Fig. 11-3

This profile of Mountain Chief helps illustrate the placement of ermine fringed hides and tubes, as well as the porcupine quilled strips that decorate the bonnet feathers. Ermine "spots" accent the feather tips.

Materials

A. Rawhide strip 5" x 30" for Headband (Substitute: millinery grade double buckram, which is a thick cotton based fabric. Get 10" x 30" so it can be folded lengthwise to make a 5" x 30" strip.)

B. Imitation Eagle Tail Feathers: 24-28 These can be all one side or half Lefts, half Rights.

C. Willow stick: Must be "green" (freshly cut), no more than ½" at the largest diameter, and 4'-6' long. (Best to gather several, in case some break during the shaping process.)

D. 1 Turkey wing spike (Substitute 3/16" x 18" wood dowel) for Pompon

E. 3-4 ozs. 5" – 6" red Strung Saddle Hackles

F. Rawhide (or thin, stiff leather) for feather loops 4½" x 8"

G. Red trade wool: 11" x 54" (or whatever the full width of a bolt of cloth is) Substitute red wool felt.

H. Calico/muslin material: 1 yd. x 6" (For inner lining of headband)

I. ½" oz. 12" – 14" red horsehair (optional)

J. 1 36" Soft leather/buckskin lace – for Primary Lace

K. 2 Bobbins heavy cotton thread (e.g., Button & Carpet thread)

L. 1 Spool of colored thread (Recommended: white or yellow) – for Firecracker thread wraps or red (only) to sew up back of Firecracker.

M. 6' – 8' Simulated Sinew: For Secondary Lace. Can substitute heavy string, such as "kite string". If Simulated Sinew is used, acquire the full-thickness type.

N. Side Drop Materials

　Note: Authentic bonnets had ermine tubes (previously discussed under Side Drops). For this bonnet, you will need approximately 6-8 white ermine hides (either cased or open skinned without heads or tails), plus a large scrap of skunk or bear fur (approximate total of 1 square foot will be more than sufficient). Also: 1 piece soft buckskin: 5"-6" x 18" (enough to cut 20 ½" x 18" thongs)

　Modern Substitute: Use strips of white rabbit fur in lieu of ermine tubes. This will require 1 large white rabbit skin with no holes (Grade A)

O. 1 Bottle of craft glue

P. 1 Roll of Masking Tape (optional)

Q. 4 1/8" x 36" Wood Dowels

R. Headband Decorations: Unlike the bonnet worn by Mountain Chief, not all examples had headband decorations directly over the forehead area. However, most examples did have something, usually a brass product. Items used were brass shoe buttons, small flat brass buttons, 2 pronged brass spots, etc. Quantities required will depend on how extensively you want to decorate your bonnet.

　As you will note in photo, the remaining areas have fringed ermine fur strips applied liberally on the sides and sometimes all along the top of the head band. This will require 6-8 additional large ermine skins (or an additional white rabbit hide) in order to include these decorations.

BASIC CONSTRUCTION

(Please read the instruction completely through before beginning.)

Refer to **Fig. 11-4 and 11-5** for the visual details to make a Straight Up bonnet.

Fig. 11-4

Inside view of completed Straight Up bonnet. Note inner cloth liner and willow hoop. This example made by and photos courtesy of Dr. Bill Holm.

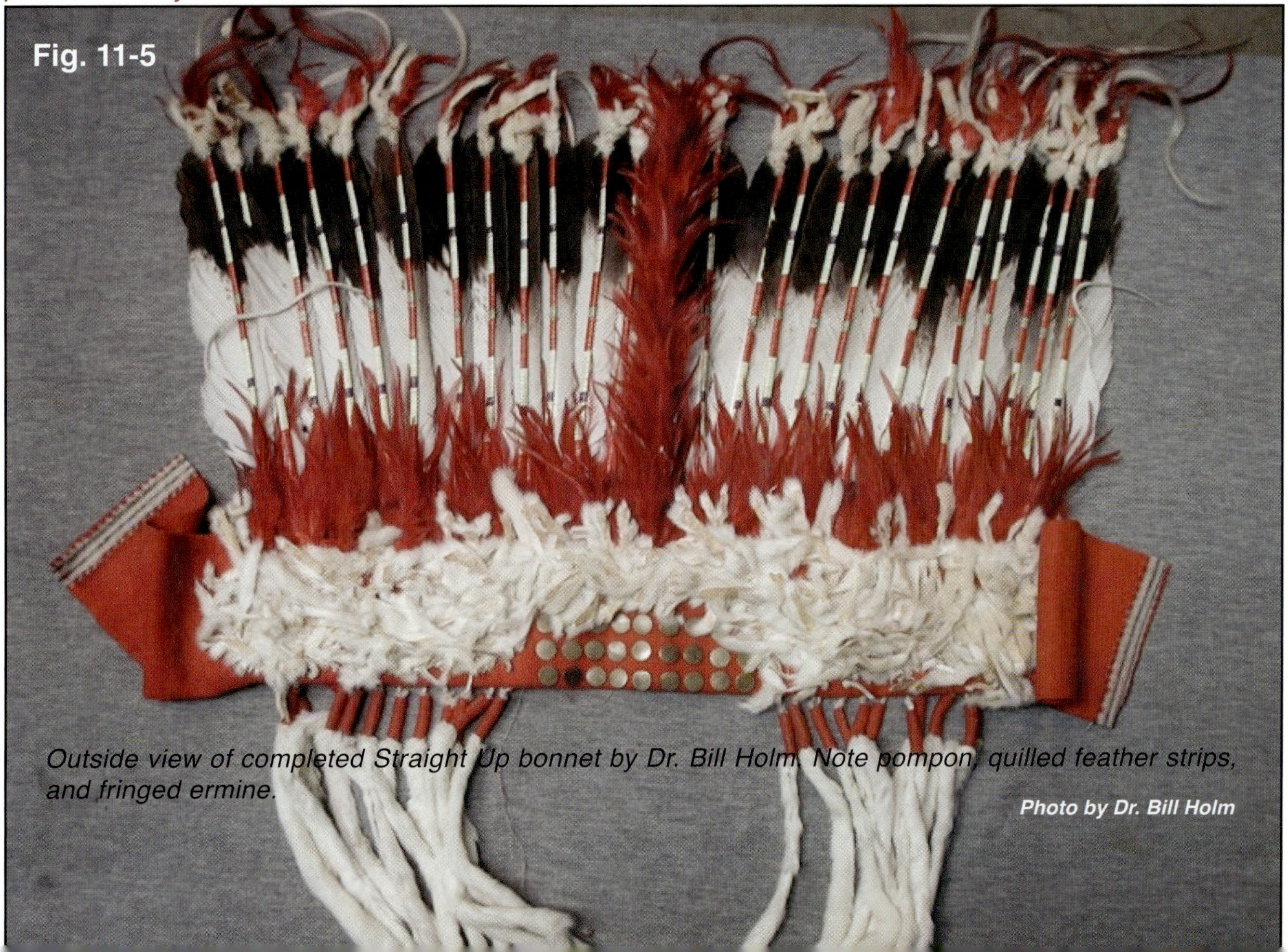

Photo by Dr. Bill Holm

Fig. 11-5

Outside view of completed Straight Up bonnet by Dr. Bill Holm. Note pompon, quilled feather strips, and fringed ermine.

Photo by Dr. Bill Holm

Feather Attachments

Across the Plains, a standard technique was commonly used in preparing and attaching feathers to the crown when constructing the basic bonnet. Specifically, a rawhide or stiff leather loop is attached to the end of each feather, and a soft thong is used to lace on each feather through small slits made in the crown. Although Straight Up bonnets sometimes employed this same technique, other methods were used which eliminated the loop, whereby feathers were stuck into head band slits or individually stitched on. Be aware of these variations whenever you examine photos of historic examples. For our purposes, we will utilize the loops and lacing method.

Willow Hoop

The Straight Up bonnet is not a "stove pipe" shape but, rather, flares slightly outward toward the top. This is achieved when a thin willow hoop is tied inside the feather circle at four places at the level of the secondary lace. The diameter of the hoop is slightly larger than the inside diameter of the finished bonnet near the top of the headband. **(See Fig. 11-4)**

Gather a straight, green piece of willow and peel the leaves and bark from it. Cut off both ends so that the resulting stick is approximately 30" long with a thickness of approximately 3/16"-1/4" at the thin end of the stick. Use a sharp knife and carefully thin down the entire stick so that it is no more than 1/4" in diameter.

As soon as the stick is of the proper dimension, it must be formed into a circle before it dries out. Use a large tin can of approx. 7" – 8" diameter as a form around which to bend the stick (or you can "eyeball it" and bend it without a form). Bend the stick around the can until the ends overlap. Then tie together the overlapped ends, re-fit the willow to the form, and allow it to dry completely. Note: The finished hoop must be both round and able to lay flat.

Set the hoop aside to dry as you work on the rest of the bonnet. Later, the hoop will be cut to its final length after the secondary lace is sewn to the feathers.

Headband

Measure the circumference of your head just above the eyebrows and cut the rawhide strip to that length plus 2". Position it on the red cloth in such a way that the cloth folds up and overlaps near the bottom. **(Fig. 11-6)** Now, whip stitch the edge of the cloth to itself from one end of the rawhide to the other. Leave the remaining ends of the cloth so they will fall free. **(Fig. 11-7)** It will be very beneficial if you use fabric glue (e.g., Aileen's Tacky Glue) to glue the fabric to both sides of the rawhide before sewing. This will prevent the fabric from moving when you mark and cut it for feather slits, etc. If you use common craft glue, be very careful not to overly saturate the fabric, which can cause unsightly hard spots on the material.

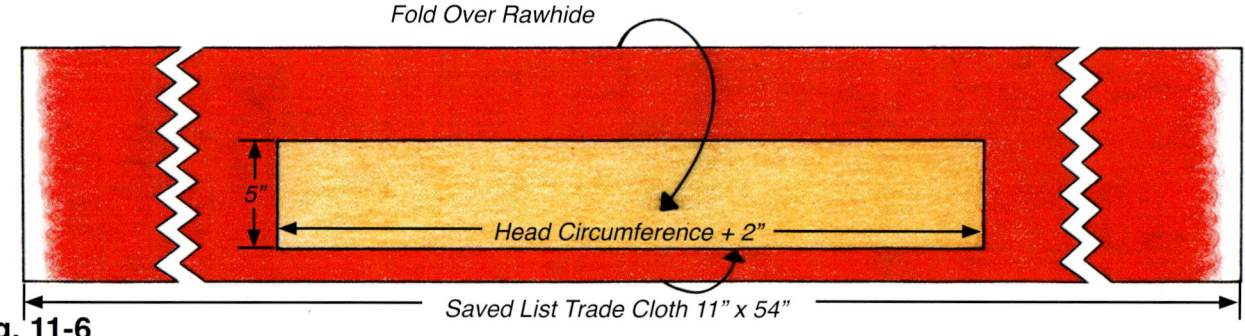

Fig. 11-6
Center the rawhide strip on the cloth but nearer the cloth's bottom edge. Fold the cloth over the rawhide to overlap itself.

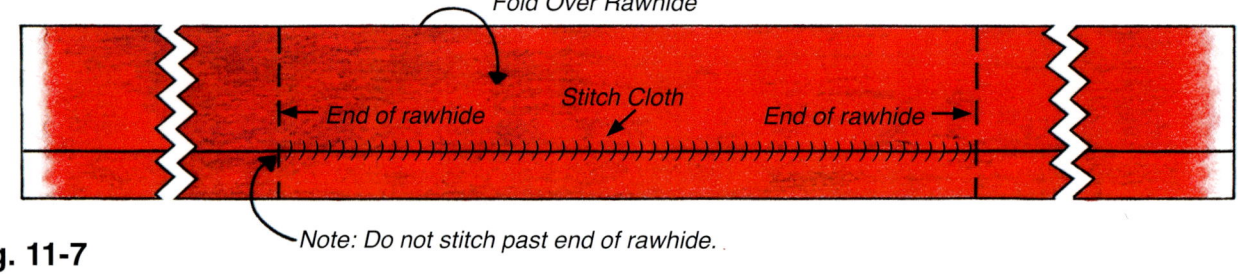

Fig. 11-7
Stitch the cloth as shown. Seam only goes from one end of the rawhide to the other.

Try on the headband and pinch the headband together at the back center of your head so that the ends are pointing back (in other words, they meet but do not overlap). Mark the band at each point where they touch. Then use a heated wire (e.g., coat hanger) to burn a pair of holes in each end of the rawhide portion so that, when a buckskin thong is inserted, you can tie the headband into a circle with the short tab ends pointing out. **(Fig. 11-8)**

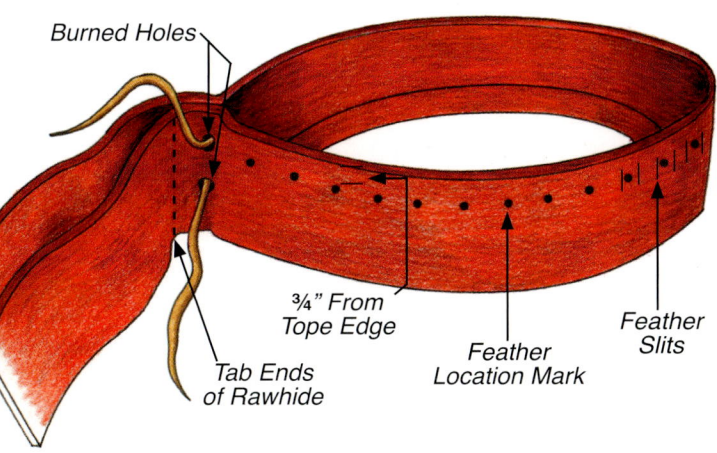

Fig. 11-8
Burn holes for leather lace so that, when tied, the headband fits your head comfortably.

Note: Perform any Headband Decorations and lace on the feathers before applying the protective inner calico (or muslin) sweat band.

Feather Placement

Before applying any decorations to the headband, you should first mark it on the front for feather placement. Place the headband on your head and tie the ends. Remove the head band and measure the distance around the band, then divide that measurement by the number of feathers. The resulting measurement (let's call it "X") will be the distance apart that the feathers will be placed. Now use a pencil and, starting at the center and ¾" from the top edge, measure and mark the band where the feathers will be located. (Remember, if using an even number of feathers, the marks for each of the front 2 feathers will only be half of "X" from the center of the headband.)

After marking, proceed with a sharp craft knife to cut the lacing slits through the cloth and rawhide. **(See Fig. 11-8)** Place a block of scrap wood beneath the headband as you make the cuts; this will give you better control to not accidentally cut the slits too long.

Headband Decoration

Look at the various photos of Straight Up bonnets in this book, as well as on-line museum sites, other books, etc. You will notice a variety of methods and trade goods used to decorate the headband. Most common is to have 2 or more rows of brass shoe buttons, small flat buttons, etc. placed on the area in front that will cover the forehead. Usually, the area decorated in front is between the temples of your forehead. Apply the chosen decorations at this time.

Another very common adornment is to have fringed strips of ermine hide sewn to the remainder of the brow band, such that the fringed pieces fall downward. You can use strips of ermine fur, cut and fringed like the Indians prepared them **(See Fig. 11-1)**, or you can substitute rabbit skin. The key detail is to cut these fur fringes approximately ¼" wide. These furred strips are placed in different ways. One common style is to sew a strip along the very top of the brow band such that, when the feathers are attached, the fringes fall down between each feather. Other furred strips are sewn to the sides of the brow band in horizontal rows, slightly overlapping. Again, study the photos to decide how you wish to decorate your headband, and then cut the fur strips and sew them on. (Be sure to allow for the feathers that will be attached at the points you marked.

To make furred strips from a cased ermine skin, first square up the top of the hide by cutting off the head. Then cut the hide down one side – **not the belly** – and lay open the hide. **(Fig. 11-9)** See the section on Ermine Tubes for how to stretch and make the hide flat. After it is dry, mark the hide horizontally in 3" sections **(Fig. 11-10)**, then make vertical marks ¼" apart between the 3" marks. Cut out the 3" sections using the cutting method described earlier, square up each section on the end so that you have a rectangle of hide, then proceed to cut the fringes. Note that the fringes will only be 2 ¾" long, so do not cut all the way from the bottom to the top of the 3" section. **(Fig. 11-11)**

Fig. 11-9
Ermine hide split down the side.

Fig. 11-10
Hide marked in 3" sections.

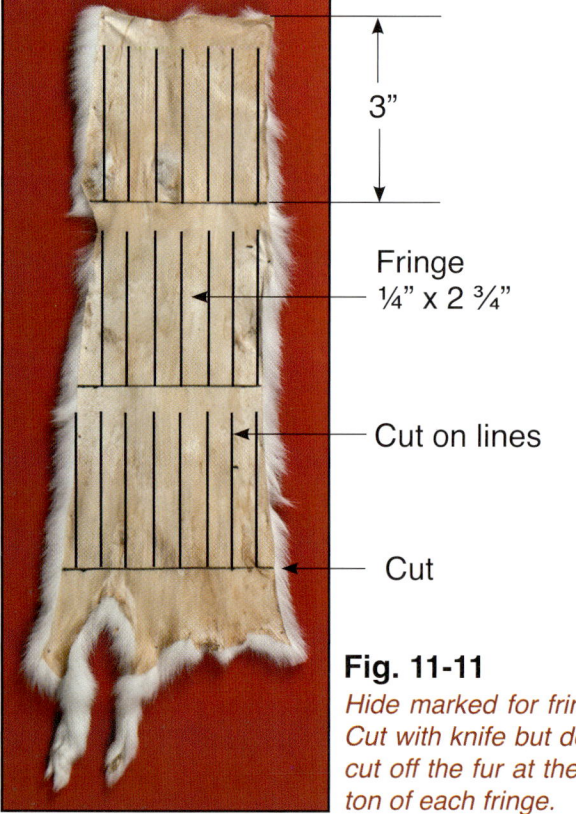

Fig. 11-11
Hide marked for fringes. Cut with knife but do not cut off the fur at the bottom of each fringe.

Sew the fringed hide strips to the headband. For overlapping layers of ermine fringe strips, first sew on the lower strips so that the bottom ends of the fringes only extend approximately ½" below the bottom edge of the head band. Sew on the other strips horizontally so they are evenly spaced and with the last strip at the top of the head band. Strips should not be placed so that they will interfere with lacing on the feathers. However, remember that many examples have the fringes dropping down between the feathers.

Ermine Tubes

See the previous discussion in this book on how to prepare ermine tubes (or rabbit strip substitutes). After preparing the tubes, they may be attached along the bottom edge of the headband, including the back. **(Fig. 11-12)** You can do this now or wait until after attaching the feathers.

Fig. 11-12

Beinecke Rare Book and Manuscript Library, Yale University

Blackfoot man dressed for warrior society dance. This view shows the horizontal layering of the ermine hide fringes on his bonnet. Photo is hand-colored glass lantern slide by Walter McClintock.

Feather Preparation

As mentioned in the materials list, the Imitation Eagle Feathers may be all from the same side or half and half. If they are half Lefts and half Rights, then they will be placed on the bonnet in the same manner as the flared Plains bonnet. However, if they are all from one side, then they will all face the same direction as they are laced in a circle around the headband. Either style can be seen in historic examples.

Prepare the Imitation Eagle Feathers as you would for a regular warbonnet, using the Feather Preparation instructions given previously. However, instead of base and tip fluffies, substitute several red hackles both at the base and tip of each feather. An added option is to apply red horsehair tassels to each tip before gluing on the hackles. These tassels should only be approximately 6" or so. Be sure that all the Imitation Eagle Feathers are extended to the same length and that the quill of each has been pierced on the back side in preparation for the secondary lace which will be applied later.

For added tip decorations, some bonnet examples show small squares of ermine hide glued over the base of the tip hackles and hair tassels. It is easiest to do this as you prepare each feather.

Deluxe Feather Decoration

In some of the accompanying photos **(See Fig. 11-1 and 11-4)**, you will note that the quill of each feather is decorated with a thin strip of porcupine quillwork. Such quillwork adds a special visual dimension to these bonnets and should be attached to the feather after the loop is affixed but before applying any other decorations. Quilled strips are tied on with thread around the base, tip, and middle of both the feather and quilled strip. See the book, *A Quillwork Companion* by Jean Heinbuch, for information on how to do quill wrapping on rawhide.

Attach The Feather

After all of the headband decorations have been applied, attach the optional pompon (see below). Then, lace on the feathers through the head band loops. When you reach each end of the headband, simply tie off the primary lace end with a knot.

Pompon

See the previous discussion on how to make a pompon using strung rooster saddle hackles. Use the turkey wing spike for this purpose by stripping the webbing, clipping off the thin tip of the quill, and straightening it. Its final length should be the same as the other bonnet feathers, so extend it if necessary. (You can substitute a 3/16" wood dowel for the wing spike.) This spike also needs to be pierced (drill the dowel with a 1/16" bit) to receive the secondary lace at the same distance from the bottom as the other feathers. As described earlier, tie on the strung saddle hackles, then apply a red wool covering (firecracker). Note: In this example, you will not include a rawhide loop.

After the headband is completed, the pompon will be the first feather attached to it. At that time, position it at the front center of the headband. Secure it by very tightly sewing it to the center of the headband, both at the top and bottom of the firecracker. Use a thin awl to poke stitching holes through the headband.

Sweat Band

(See Fig. 11-4) Cut a piece of calico (or muslin) 6" wide and the length of the rawhide strip plus 1". Fold under ½" all the way around the edges and iron this material flat. Then whip stitch it to the wool on the inside of the headband so that it forms a liner covering the wool and primary lacing.

With an awl and using the pairs of lace holes at each end of the headband as guides, poke holes all the way through the material.

Finishing Up

String the feathers together with the secondary lace by starting at the pompon and working towards the back on each side. Now, insert the buckskin tie thong and tie together the ends of the headband. Loosely tie the ends of the secondary lace. Have someone else wear the bonnet while you adjust the spacing of the feathers along the secondary lace. Remember that the bonnet will have a slight flare, and so adjust the feathers and lace accordingly. When you are satisfied with the spacing, tie the ends of the secondary lace loosely.

For the willow hoop, use the measurement of the inside circumference of the headband (when it is tied together in a circle) and add 2" to that dimension. Then overlap and tie the ends of the willow together so that its finished circumference has that dimension.

Now, take the willow hoop and attach four short leather thongs to it at equal spaces. Insert the hoop into the bonnet, then tie the hoop to the secondary lace at those four positions. The bonnet should now have a slight flare at the top with the feathers spaced evenly. Make any adjustments to the feathers as necessary, then securely tie the ends of the secondary lace to each other and trim the excess.

Straight Up Trailer Bonnets

There are many historic examples of Straight Up bonnets with single trailers. **(Fig. 11-13 & Fig. 11-14)** The trailer is attached to the back of the headband and constructed in the fashion of the previously described Plains trailer bonnets. Although the author was not able to examine actual specimens, apparently, the top end of the secondary lace is secured to the back of the headband, as opposed to tying it to the secondary lace of the headband feathers.

Denver Public Library, Western History Collection

Fig. 11-13 *Joseph Lelps-to, Flathead. ca. 1900-1910. This view illustrates a typical Straight Up bonnet with eagle feather trailer. Note the gap between the top trailer feather and the actual bonnet crown feathers.*

Fig. 11-14 *Blackfoot dancers. Man on left has a Straight Up trailer bonnet, again showing a separation between the actual trailer and the bonnet crown feathers.*

Buffalo Bill Historical Center, Cody, Wyoming, U.S.A.; Gift of Robert F. Garland, NA.205.15

Oglala Sioux Single Trailer Warbonnet, ca. 1880. Belonged to Chief Little Wound who died August 18, 1891. The trailer's primary lace is broken, and so the trailer feathers are no longer attached to the crown feathers. Typical of so many bonnets, the crown is a felt skull cap to which is attached a lane-stitched brow band. Side drops are clusters of loose hawk feathers. For the trailer, red saved list wool trade cloth was backed with canvas which helps the trailer keep its flat shape. The war bonnet has no base plumes or tip decorations, thus accenting the full beauty of the natural immature golden eagle tail feathers.

Summary 12

Like all topics within the study of the Native American, the breadth of information on warbonnets is vast. And for those wishing to recreate this or any material culture object of these peoples, there is also a responsibility. This entails learning as much as possible about the object, including its history, meaning, development, and variations among different tribes – all in addition to how to make it. Unlike recreational arts and crafts with no ties to a particular culture, those who make reproductions of Indian pieces – whether historic or modern versions – owe it to the native artists who have gone before to show them respect by learning as much as possible before attempting to make these recreations. With the hope of introducing readers to the many dimensions of this fascinating piece of Indian culture, *The Plains Indian Warbonnet: Its Story and Construction* was written.

This book has but scratched the surface of the subject of the American Indian warbonnet, and the author hopes it will be the springboard for readers to delve deeper into how and why they were used and made.

The "crown of feathers" which now can broadly be referred to as the warbonnet likely had its origin among a number of tribes, all in pre-contact times with Europeans. As settlers moved west, they continued to encounter indigenous peoples who used raptor feathers attached to a skullcap as part of their war and ceremonial attire. A number of artists in the early 1800s captured images of western Indians using what we today think of as the Plains warbonnet. And, over time and with the help of photography, we can see that the warbonnet evolved into several distinct styles. By the Indian Wars Period, more than one style would be observed worn by men of the same tribe. This is one facet that shows that, like most Indian material culture specimens, the bonnet encompassed the latitude for individual taste, the use and availability of a variety of decorative components, and special significance which, in the mind of the wearer, imbued him with perceived power above that of mortal man.

With the onset of the reservation, the railroad and live entertainment shows helped introduce non-Indians to the fascinating peoples about whom they had only read. Tourists came to the Indians, and Indians came to the so-called "civilized world" in Wild West shows that toured Eastern states and many European countries. From these experiences, the most lasting impression was that of a warrior and his warbonnet. Consequently, many tribes for whom the warbonnet was not originally part of their culture adapted this headgear to attract tourists and give added credibility that they, too, were Native American warriors.

Today, there still is widespread interest in the American Indian. A friend recently observed that it is probable that most every American household has some item, if only a trinket, that represents Indians. For non-Indians, Scouting and the Indian Hobby serve as vehicles for learning about Indian material culture and ways. And anyone who recently has traveled to areas where Indian people still live and congregate can attest that the Indian powwow is alive and well in contemporary form. Also, the warbonnet can still be seen among Indian people. Most likely, it is worn by a military veteran or other person of distinction. In this manner, the warbonnet is still given respect, and it therefore is the responsibility of anyone who makes and uses a warbonnet to treat it in kind.

Photo Gallery

Today, there are many craftsmen —both Native American and non-Indian — who make warbonnets. From these makers, we have chosen to feature the work of several individuals who demonstrate a high degree of craftsmanship while maintaining the integrity of Plains warbonnet traditions. The bonnets in this Gallery also exhibit the combination of study and experience that the artist brought to the making of each piece. Most often the craftsman will tell you that he has not copied a specific historical bonnet but, rather, created one that is representative of warbonnets of a particular tribe and time period. We hope you will enjoy studying these exceptional works of the warbonnet art.

John V. Jones has enjoyed a lifelong interest in the material culture of Native Americans which began in earnest at a young age in the 1950s in Anadarko, Oklahoma. It was there that he was introduced to the then 102 year old Hunting Horse, a distinguished Kiowa. In the last half of the 1800s, Hunting Horse had been a warrior and cavalry scout, and his knowledge and practice of the "old ways" deeply impressed John. Later, John's business travels afforded opportunities to observe and study countless examples of early headdresses in North American and European museums and private collections. He is a prolific maker of warbonnets and is most interested in historical examples that stray from the expected. He is currently retired in Chattanooga, Tennessee. All photos by John V. Jones

John dyed the hand painted imitation eagle feathers in this single trailer creation which is in a style representative of a Plains bonnet of the Indian Wars and Reservation periods. Materials used include beads in old colors for the lane stitched brow band, horsehair, red dyed ermine "spots" for the feather tips, red dyed imitation hawk feathers for side drops along with ribbons, and a leather skull cap.

Double Trailer Warbonnet   By John V. Jones

This double trailer bonnet has characteristics introduced in the late 1800s-early 1900s which are still seen today. The remarkable feature is the fully beaded feather decorations, done by wrapping strung beads in a continuous manner with intermittent stitches to anchor the beadwork. Beaded feathers are sometimes seen on Southern Plains bonnets, often done in gourd stitch. Beaded rosettes and a loomed brow are common modern touches.

Natural Turkey Tail Feather Warbonnet
By John V. Jones

This handsome warbonnet is made from natural turkey tail feathers. Though not used in historic Plains bonnets, these feathers are attractive materials readily available today. The natural colors and patterns in the feathers make a striking modern bonnet.

Joel Hendricks

Joel, 71, went to his first powwow in 1955 in Wisconsin and presently lives in Clinton, IL where he is a member of Tecumseh Lodge. He has long been active in Hobbyist circles and usually can be seen at the National Powwows. Joel is an award-winning non-Native beadworker and dollmaker, and, besides warbonnets (of which he has made 24 to date), he makes moccasins, claw necklaces, and clubs. This warbonnet was commissioned by the late Bill Marlott, Comanche, who loved to wear Crow-style clothes. Photos by Joel E. Hendricks.

One notable feature of this warbonnet is the geometric Crow-style design in the applique' beaded brow band. There are relatively few historic collected examples of Crow-made bonnets with these kinds of designs. Fringed ermine hide covers the crown, and white rooster hackles decorate the feather tips, along with yellow horse-hair tassels and ermine spots.

Mark Miller

Mark Miller is an extraordinary artisan particularly known throughout the Indian artifacts collector market for his ability to restore old pieces. But he also makes museum quality reproductions and has dedicated himself to the study and authentic restoration and recreation of material culture items. Mark is a graphics artist by training, and he and his wife, Mary, live in Kalispell, Montana. Photos by Mark Miller.

This Single Trailer Warbonnet of hand-painted feathers was created by Mark in the generic style of many Plains trailer bonnets, and, as such, does not represent a particular tribe. Prolific use was made of fringed ermine hides to decorate the crown, including fringes that peek between the feather wraps on the front of the bonnet. Attention to historic detail includes the use of material in a period-correct pattern for fabric binding on the trailer.

Joe Rosenthal

Joe Rosenthal Like many non-Indian Hobbyists, Joe became acquainted with Indian lore in Scouting. There, he learned about Indian material culture and began making items, particularly warbonnets. Joe's imagination allows him to take kits, then modify or substitute for some kit materials to make exceptional bonnets. Or he'll gather individual craft components – such as hand-painted feathers or the quillwork he's done – to create other headdresses. Joe lives in California and collaborates with Mike Tucker to produce written materials on Indian crafts and regalia to introduce Scouts and others to the Indian hobby. All photos by Joe Rosenthal.

In this example, Joe has taken a basic kit from Crazy Crow Trading Post and made substitutions and changes to produce a more historic looking product. He made a lane stitched beaded brow band and substituted shell discs for the beaded rosettes in the kit. And, like many historic examples, the firecrackers have no bands of thread wraps.

The excellent look achieved in this bonnet was in large part the result of careful straightening, extending, and trimming of production-grade imitation eagle feathers.

Hand-painted imitation eagle and red tail hawk feathers were used by Joe to create this warbonnet.

Deluxe hand-painted feathers acquired from a different craftsman than the bonnet on the left were used in combination with a brow band of porcupine quillwork to make this beautiful Sioux style warbonnet.

The bonnet at left has not only a finely quilled brow band, but Joe made porcupine quilled strips which were spot-stitched to each hand-painted feather. The photo above shows the bonnet feathers in the course of production. You can see that the quilled strips were attached before tip decorations were applied.

Kevin Stillinger

Kevin Stillinger is a young craftsman from South Carolina who makes Indian-style products to order and for on-line auction. This beautiful bonnet is another example of taking non-traditional-looking feathers to create an artistic piece of work. Kevin used Royal Palm turkey wing feathers, which bring to mind the look of real bald eagle feathers. He's also incorporated a fine lane stitched beaded browband from which are suspended another traditional trade item: hawk bells. Photos by Kevin Stillinger.

Dave Hagstrom

Dave is a professional artist in Byron, Wyoming who also specializes in Indian-style crafts. In this example, he has achieved a real old-time look. Dave used buffalo horn which he thinned and polished, then decorated the tips. The creation of this warbonnet was inspired by several old examples from the 19th century Northern Plains. It is now owned by a contemporary western artist and used in his paintings because of its historical accuracy. Photos courtesy of Dave Hagstrom.

Foreign Artifacts

Since the 1700s, Indian artifacts were collected by foreign visitors to America and now reside in museums around the world. The warbonnets on this page and the next are in Germany, and, although the makers were not recorded, they appear to be Northern Plains pieces from the first half of the 1900s. This first example is in the typical flared style. Although the brow band has tipi/mountain designs common to many tribes, the colors and geometric layout lend themselves to a Crow attribution. In the yellow section, two shades of yellow beads were used, something not uncommon with Indian beadwork when the craftsperson had limited supplies. Brass shoe buttons also decorate the brow band.

Photos courtesy of Ottoneum Museum, Kassel, Germany.

Photos courtesy of Ottoneum Museum, Kassel, Germany.

Pen & ink drawing by Frank Knickerbocker from an early photo

Above Photo: Two Moons (Ishaynishus), Northern Cheyenne, early 1900s. This drawing by Frank Knickerbocker was done from a photograph of this famous Cheyenne chief. Two Moons (1847 – 1917) was one of the Cheyenne leaders at the Battle of the Little Big Horn and the Battle of the Rosebud. After surrender, he became a scout for Gen. Nelson Miles. Two Moons was also one of the two models for the "buffalo" nickel produced by the U.S. Mint. The drawing shows Mr. Knickerbocker's exceptional portraiture skill and ability to capture the look of eagle feathers.

Left Facing Page: This is a Double Trailer example with the trailer material having been split half-way up the back. The trailer feathers are continuations of the circle of feathers on the crown. A nice decoration at the top of the trailer split is a small amount of beadwork. Gypsum or clay was dabbed on the feather tips.

Acknowledgements

The author wishes to thank and acknowledge the following, without whose help this book would not have been possible:

Randy Brewer
Sean Campbell, Buffalo Bill Historical Center
Allen Chronister
Dave Hagstrom
Joel Hendricks
Dr. Bill Holm
John V. Jones
Bud Lake
Benson Lanford
Mark Miller
Paul Raczka
J. Rex Reddick
Matt Reed, Curator, Oklahoma History Museum
Joe Rosenthal
Ellen Sieber, Mathers Museum
Kevin Stillinger
Chas Weldon, Yellowstone County Museum

Bibliography

Bates, Craig D. *A Plateau Style War Bonnet.* Moccasin Tracks, Vol. 8 No. 1. 1982.
Johnson, Michael G. *Blackfeet Bonnet.* Whispering Wind Vol. 24, No. 6. 1991.
LaRocque, Francoise. *The Journal of Larocque from the Assiniboine to the Yellowstone 1805.* Publications of the Canadian Archives, No. 3. Ottawa Government Printing Bureau. 1910.
Peate, Rod. *Warbonnets.*   Published by Crazy Crow Trading Post. 1984.
Shawley, Stephen Douglas. *Nez Perce Dress, A study of Cultural Change.* University of Idaho. 1974.
Thompson, James "Putt". Personal conversations. 2010.
Wissler, Clark. *Material Culture of the Blackfoot Indians,* Anthropological Papers of the American Museum of Natural History V (I). 1910.